Ben Cropp

blood in the water

By Mike Colman

as told to him by Ben Cropp

PARK
STREET
PRESS

Published jointly by
Park Street Press
(a division of ACP Magazines Ltd (ABN 18 053 273 546) and
Media 21 Publishing Pty Ltd (ABN 82 090 635 073)

ACP Magazines Ltd
54 Park Street, Sydney, GPO Box 4088, Sydney, NSW 1028

Media21 Publishing Pty Ltd
30 Bay Street, Double Bay, NSW 2028
Tel: (02) 9362 1800 Fax: (02) 9362 9500
Email: m21@media21.com.au`
Website: www.media21publishing.com

National Library of Australia Cataloguing-in-Publication entry

Cropp, Ben, 1936- .
Ben Cropp : blood in the water.

ISBN 1 876624 67 1.

1. Cropp, Ben, 1936- . 2. Skin divers - Australia -
Biography. 3. Underwater exploration. I. Colman, Mike.
II. Title.

797.23092

Designer Michelle Wiener
Photographs Ben Cropp
Additional photographs Lynn Cropp Dean Cropp
John Harding Rhonda Smith Ron Taylor

Editor Carol Cromie
Colour reproduction Clayton Lloyd
Printed by Phoenix Offset and Bookbuilders, Hong Kong
Sales Stephen Balme email: stephen@media21.com.au

Ben Cropp, the smiling diver.

contents

 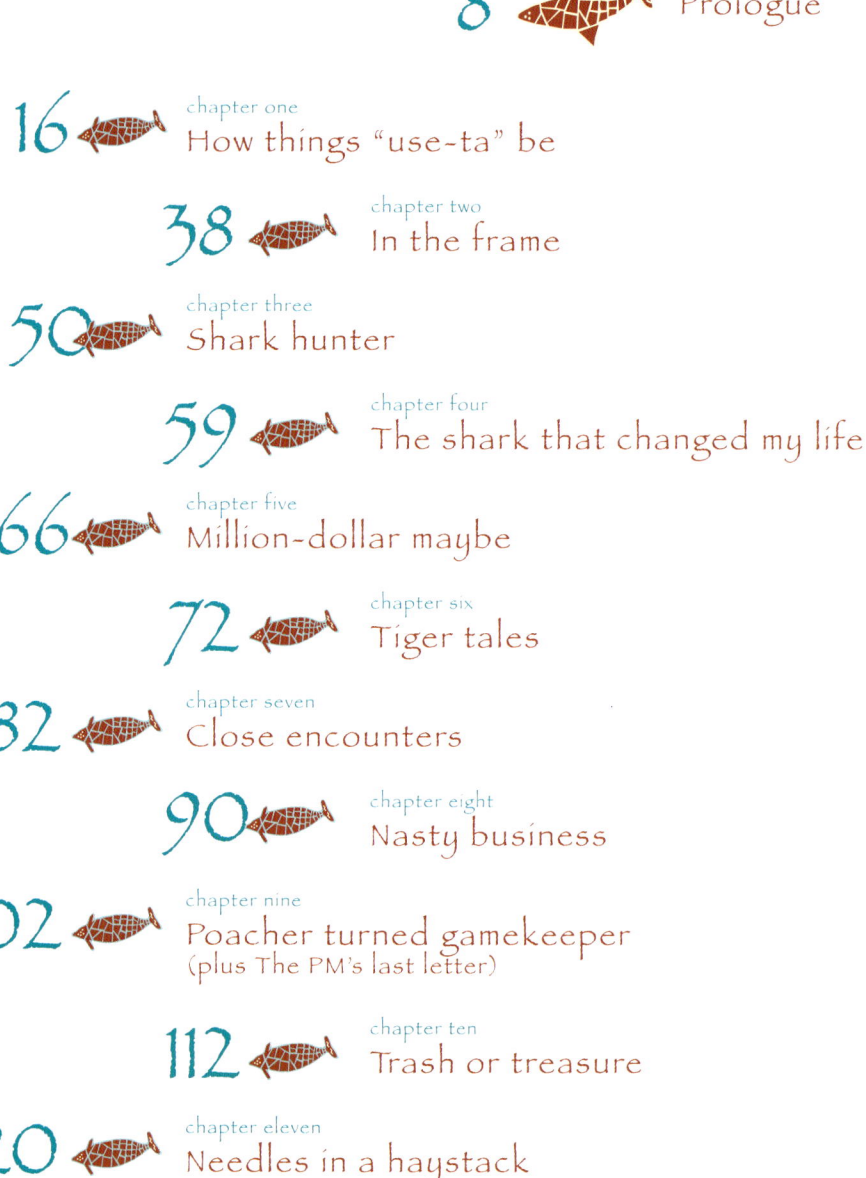

Prologue

In the beginning (opposite): Skotolan, Buka in the Solomon Islands where I was born; as a baby with my siblings in 1936; as a youngster in Casino; with Australian Cinematographers Awards for wildlife films at Port Douglas. This page: the Australian Open Spearfishing Champion with trophy in 1961; as a 17-year-old with record-sized 100-pound (45-kilo) cod taken off Byron Bay; leading the Australian contingent of spearfishers in Sicily.

THE TIGER shark had disappeared. We were sitting in our rubber dinghy at Batt Reef, three adults and a dog, looking for all the world like kids in a swimming pool waiting for a mate to tip us out so we could laugh and scream in mock fright. But there was nothing to laugh about this time, and nothing mock about the fear in the air as the tiger shark made its move.

For almost a lifetime I had been swimming among man-killers. I had hunted them and filmed them, and in nearly every case, I had felt totally in control of the situation. This was different. This time it was the shark, and not me or my companions, who had the upper hand. We were unarmed; we had no 303-calibre bullet-head spear, no vial of deadly poison, no gun, just a camera. Most worrying of all, I couldn't see where the shark was and, in 55 years of diving alongside some of the deadliest creatures on the planet, my number one rule had been: always keep them in sight.

From the day I took my first dive, wearing a homemade mask and carrying a spear with a point hammered by the local blacksmith, I had been captivated by the world under the sea. What started out as a hobby developed into an obsession and then into a career. Over the years I had become Australia's most successful maker of nature documentaries. I found more historic shipwrecks in Australian waters than anyone else and I won international awards for my photography. Yet mention my name to most

Australians and they'll say, "Oh, the shark bloke."

It's true that sharks were my entry into the business of filmmaking. The public's fascination with sharks at a time when they were known as nothing more than killing machines catapulted me to the forefront of a fledgling industry. The day I decided to become a filmmaker was the day I became a shark hunter. If the public wanted to see sharks up close, jaws snapping and tails thrashing in a frenzy of blood lust, then that's what I would give them. If they wanted to see sharks being killed simply because it looked

With my first underwater movie camera preparing to make the film Shark Safari *in 1963.*

A big tiger shark circles a coral cay looking for turtles; with an Australian-record-sized coral cod I speared at Lady Elliot Island on the Great Barrier Reef.

spectacular on their TV screens, I would give them that too. In the context of my career, my time as a shark killer was a mere blink of an eye, but it was a blink that would stay with me forever.

People tend to forget about the other things I've done: the many adventure films I made, my historic Shipwreck Museum at Port Douglas in Far North Queensland, and my internationally recognised work as a conservationist. And sharks were just one of many deadly creatures I came face to face with over the years. There were sea snakes and crocodiles, and I even exposed myself to the poison of the box jellyfish to test its potency. I faced other dangers, too: for instance, I nearly drowned when I got trapped under a boulder during a white-water-rafting adventure gone wrong.

Still, no-one could help but be affected, amused even, if I happened now to meet my end in the jaws of a crazed, man-eating tiger shark, and here at Batt Reef, east-north-east of Port Douglas, it looked as if I might just be headed that way.

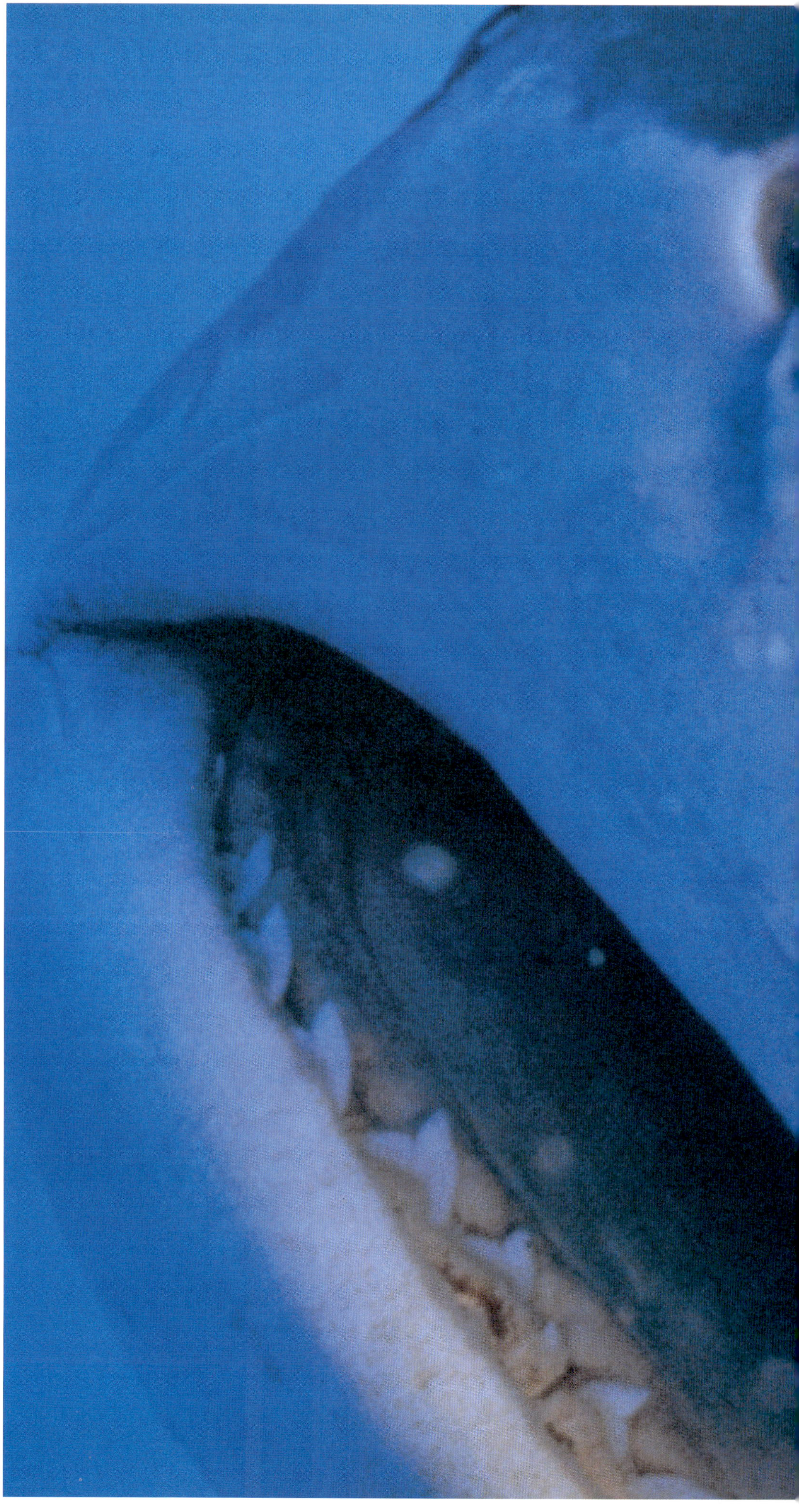

This four-metre tiger shark was intent on biting my camera, and was only half a metre away when I got this picture.

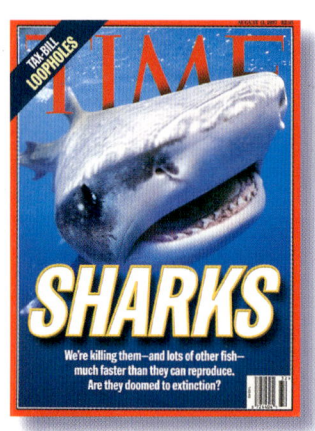

The eye of the tiger: the photo (right) that I snapped half a metre away from the jaws of a 4m tiger shark as it swam past my dinghy made the cover of "Time" magazine in 1997, above. Above right, a tiger shark bites into my dinghy at Batt Reef. John Harding, who took this photo, Trina Fleischmann, Tuffy the dog and I were in the dinghy at the time.

We peered about us, scanning the water from one side of the dinghy to the other, searching for the shark's fin, but nothing. There was only one place the shark could be - directly underneath the dinghy and sizing us up.

Just as we realised this, the shark launched itself upwards with a snap of its massive jaws in a curtain of white water. As one of my companions leapt sideways, the shark's teeth shredded the hard plastic casing of the dinghy's inflatable pontoon just centimetres from where she'd been sitting. The shark snapped again and again, and began shaking its head from side to side as the air escaped from the pontoon and the dinghy listed dangerously. The more the shark struggled, the more it became obvious why it hadn't retreated when it realised the dinghy was not some tasty morsel. Its razor-sharp teeth had become caught in the PVC casing of the pontoon, which was now being ripped away as the shark tried frantically to free itself. With every ferocious lunge, it damaged the dinghy further, and pulled us ever closer to those horrible teeth.

What could possibly have turned this deadly yet calculating creature into a blind, maniacal killing machine? My mind flashed back to a group of Torres Strait Islander fishermen we had passed a few minutes earlier. They had just speared a turtle and were pulling it into their boat. The tiger shark wasn't after us; it was after the turtle. That was what had sent it crazy, turning it into a potential man-killer.

It had smelled blood. Blood in the water, the story of my life …

How things "use-ta" be

All in the family: my son Adam scuba dives with camera (and companion); and, right, my second wife, Eva, swims gamely by a dangerous whaler shark in 1967.

F I WERE to give myself a nickname, it would be "Use-ta", as in "I use-ta catch huge barramundi just off that reef" or "We use-ta dive wherever we wanted without any pushy bureaucrats telling us what to do." The older I get the more I find myself using the phrase, but when I think back on the things I have seen and done in more than 55 years of adventure, in the sea and out, it is hard not to think about how different things "use-ta" be.

When I started diving in 1950 the skindiving industry didn't exist. There was no scuba gear; even snorkels weren't available. By today's standards, the equipment we used was crude to say the least. Often we

With mate Jimmy Carruthers and a flathead speared in the Tweed River in 1953; a Louisiade Archipelago islander stuns a massive crayfish; an emperor angelfish.

made things up as we went along. Today's divers with all their state-of-the-art scuba and wetsuits would probably feel sorry for us. They shouldn't. The things we saw for the very first time, the untouched undersea landscapes teeming with fish life, will never be seen again.

Those of us venturing underwater in those early days were part of a privileged group. I thank my lucky stars I was born when I was – even though my first dive, at the age of three, was almost my last.

My family was living on the island of Buka in the Solomon Islands (now Bougainville) where my father, Allan Herbert Cropp, was a Methodist missionary. I was born there in January 1936. My mother, Louise, named me Benjamin because in Hebrew it means "last of the tribe", but it proved a misnomer. I would be the fifth of seven children, three boys and four girls. Only Joan, the eldest, was Australia-born.

We lived in a mission house by the sea at a place called Skotalan and it was there that I was first drawn to the water – literally. I was walking along the beach with my older brothers and sisters when I discovered a small coral pool. Wondering what was happening below the surface, I bent down and promptly fell in. Luckily Joan was able to haul me out before I drowned, and I've been diving headfirst into the sea ever since.

When my father's time in the islands came to an end, we moved to Lennox Head, then just a little seaside village on the far north coast of New South Wales. It was here in my early teens that I developed my love of fishing. With my friend, Barry Stewart, a classmate at Ballina High School, I spent every spare moment fishing off the beach with a rod and reel. The fishing was good in those days – Barry's father once caught a 90-pound (41-kilo) jewfish and walked more than a kilometre and a half home with it over his shoulder. Like all fishermen, Barry and I were always on the lookout for a way to increase our chances of a good haul. In January 1950, at age 14, I saw something that would change my life forever.

A group of Torres Strait Islanders from a mission were diving at the mouth of the Richmond River at Ballina, just south of Lennox Head, and they were doing what I had never seen before – spearfishing.

They wore little pairs of goggles and had hand spears. I was totally hooked. "Gee," I thought. "That's a novel way to catch fish." And just then one of them came to the surface with a big flathead, much bigger than anything Barry or I could hope to catch off the Broadwater. I headed straight to Barry's house and told him what I had seen. We didn't hesitate. If this was a good way to catch fish, we wanted to try it. In Lennox Head in 1950, you didn't just walk into a sports store, point to the goggles or flippers that you liked the look of and hand over your credit card. Such

equipment didn't exist, not that Barry and I were too concerned about that. Even if it had been available we wouldn't have been able to afford it. So, as kids did in those days, we made our own. We made masks using the inner tube from a motorbike tyre, cut some glass to see through, and held it all together with a copper strip. The masks were crude, but they turned out to be amazingly good.

For the spears, we went to the local blacksmith who made us some metal heads with barbs on a six-millimetre steel rod a metre and a half long. We went back to the inner tube to make a catapult.

Then, all we had to do was head down to the channel at Lennox Head and start spearing fish until we had too many to carry home. Well, that was the intention, but it wasn't quite that simple. We didn't have flippers, there was no such thing as a snorkel and our catapult spear wasn't even remotely accurate. Plus, we had no idea of the correct way to fish underwater. We thought the aim was to get close to the fish, when in reality it was all about getting the fish to come close to us. The man who put us on the right track was my history teacher, Bill Abbott, who happened to see us down at the channel one afternoon. He had learned to dive a few years earlier in Sydney and told us to stop chasing the fish and let them come to us. He told us about lead weight belts and the importance of patience. Once again, Barry and I turned to our workshop, making lead weights, which we tied to any old belts we could get our hands on. Pretty soon the fish would come up for a closer look at these strange creatures lying on the bottom of the sea, and we would spear them.

It was a turning point for me in more ways than one. As well as providing the next step in a lifelong love affair with the underwater world, it enabled me to take a more responsible role in my family. For the first time, I was able to become a provider. The fish I was taking home most days made a welcome feed for a large and far from well-off family. My father, who earned little as the minister of a parish, had caught tuberculosis in the islands and was often forced to take time off work to recover from recurring bouts. We grew our own vegetables and, together with what I

Jewels of the sea:
soft red coral with
reef fish all around.

A crown of thorns starfish (left) devours coral polyps, leaving only a white skeleton; I killed this nine-foot (2.8-metre) grey nurse shark with a barb-less spear at Brush Island, NSW in 1962 (photo by Ron Taylor); a Laughlan Islander with a barracuda to celebrate my first trip back in 20 years.

could catch, we never went hungry. The feeling of independence, which came from being able to hunt and catch my own food, has never left me and, on all my adventures over the years, I have made a point of living off the sea's bounty.

While we were never rich, we weren't poor, certainly not in terms of being a close and happy family anyway. Dad was transferred to different parishes along the NSW coast in towns like Bellingen, Ballina and Casino, and living by the sea was paradise for a kid like me.

When Dad bought a one-hectare property at Lennox Head it provided us with a wonderful place in which to grow up. By today's standards our lifestyle was basic, but it was also healthy, safe and enormous fun. There was no crime in the area, there were no drugs and nobody locked their doors. When the Lennox Head property was eventually sold and the family moved just north to Tweed Heads on the Gold Coast, Dad settled for the princely sum of $1,200. Recently, the same piece of land sold to a developer for $2.5 million. Poor Dad would be turning in his grave, but back then none of us thought of that little farmlet as a potential goldmine. To us it was just a special place to live, an idyllic environment that I tried to recreate many years later for my two children, Dean and Adam.

Barry and I continued to fine-tune our spearfishing technique and equipment. Eventually we got around to trying flippers and we never stopped tinkering with our spears to improve their accuracy. The catapults on the first spears we made were powered by two rubber strips, which had to be pulled back in exact unison or they would be uneven and off-target. There was also the risk of a strip flinging back and hitting the diver. After experimenting with various techniques, we designed a single surgical rubber tube slingshot, which is identical to the system used today.

Another of our innovations was a spear gun, which, I confess, involved minor larceny. When we had finished our blueprint, the one thing we could not manufacture from available parts was a trigger mechanism. With necessity being the mother of invention, we took a train to Byron Bay and

Big game: that's me at age 17 with a 22-pound (10-kilo) blue parrotfish I speared at Cook Island off Tweed Heads; the luminous red-and-gold beauty of reef life.

Bigger game still: I speared this world-record 90-pound (41-kilo) black kingfish at Cudgen Reef, Kingscliff, NSW, in 1957; Adam and his girlfriend Kat in scuba mode. Photo by Dean Cropp.

back, and "borrowed" two latches from a carriage window. These made perfect triggers.

The early 1950s were an exciting time for the emerging sport of spearfishing. In coastal areas all over the world people just like us were experimenting with new ways to dive and fish deeper, longer and with greater accuracy and safety. In 1953 scuba tanks became available and the first great diver-personalities such as Hans Hass and Jacques Cousteau became known to a whole generation of wannabe adventurers – including one Ben Cropp.

From the moment I picked up his book *Under the Red Sea*, Hans Hass became my hero. He still is, and we have become close friends. While not as well-known now as Cousteau, Hass was the ultimate underwater photographer and adventurer. For me, a keen amateur diver headed with limited enthusiasm towards a life as a schoolteacher, Hass seemed to have the perfect lifestyle. Whenever a new Hass book was published I would pore over it, reading and re-reading the adventures of the Austrian-born diver as he sailed the world with his gorgeous wife, Lotte. To me, they were like movie stars, the Tarzan and Jane of the underwater world. I dreamed of doing the same as Hans, travelling the world with my wife by my side. In time, I did just that (although I went through a few Lottes along the way and married three times).

In the mid-1950s, however, the chances of living like Hans and Lotte were so far from reality that I might as well have aspired to being elected Prime Minister of England. I finished my schooling at Ballina High in 1952, took the next year off to go diving and in 1954 attended Brisbane Teachers College. Within three years, I was teaching at a one-teacher school in the village of Colville, engaged to be married … and wondering what the heck I was doing.

As far as my career was concerned, the future didn't seem all that exciting. After all, where do you go from being the head of a one-teacher school? Head of a two-teacher school? Romantically, things were better, but only just. Janie, the girl I was engaged to, was sweet and beautiful – she

Close-up of a killer: a huge tiger shark makes its presence felt.
Photo by Lynn Cropp.

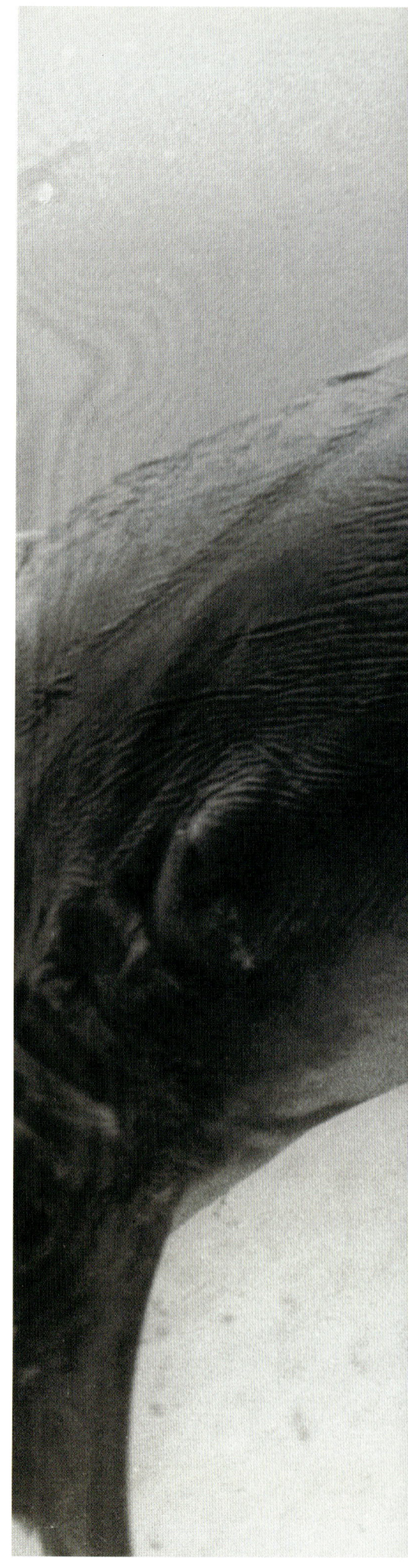

had even been crowned Miss Gold Coast – but the truth was I just wasn't ready to be tied down. Janie's mother told her I would never be anything but a beach bum, and how right she was. Today, as I sit barefoot on the veranda of my home at Port Douglas, looking down on my 17.5-metre catamaran cruiser *Freedom III* and planning my next expedition, I am indeed a beach bum. Just an upmarket one.

As my wedding day approached, I felt trapped. In those days, one didn't break off an engagement; it was seen as the ultimate black mark. Yet, much as I cared for Janie, I felt the pull of the ocean more strongly than ever.

My family had moved to Tweed Heads in 1953, and I had read that the first-ever Australian Spearfishing Championships were to be held right there on our local beach. By then I was a competent "spearo", but I had no idea how good I might be because I had never tested myself against anyone else. To me, spearfishing was just as the name implied: a way to catch fish for the table. Still, with the blind confidence of youth, I joined the Queensland Spearfishing Association and entered the Queensland team trials. With my homemade mask and spear, I scored well and was selected for the team. I was by far the youngest – our number one, Frank Kirkham, was eight years my senior – and the others, Ron Cox and John Reynolds, weren't much younger. These three were among the best spearfishermen in the country. Like me, they were self-taught, but they had experience on their side. Diving with them was a huge learning curve for me. There is no better way to learn than diving with a skilful partner and, by the time the championships came along, we had developed into a strong team.

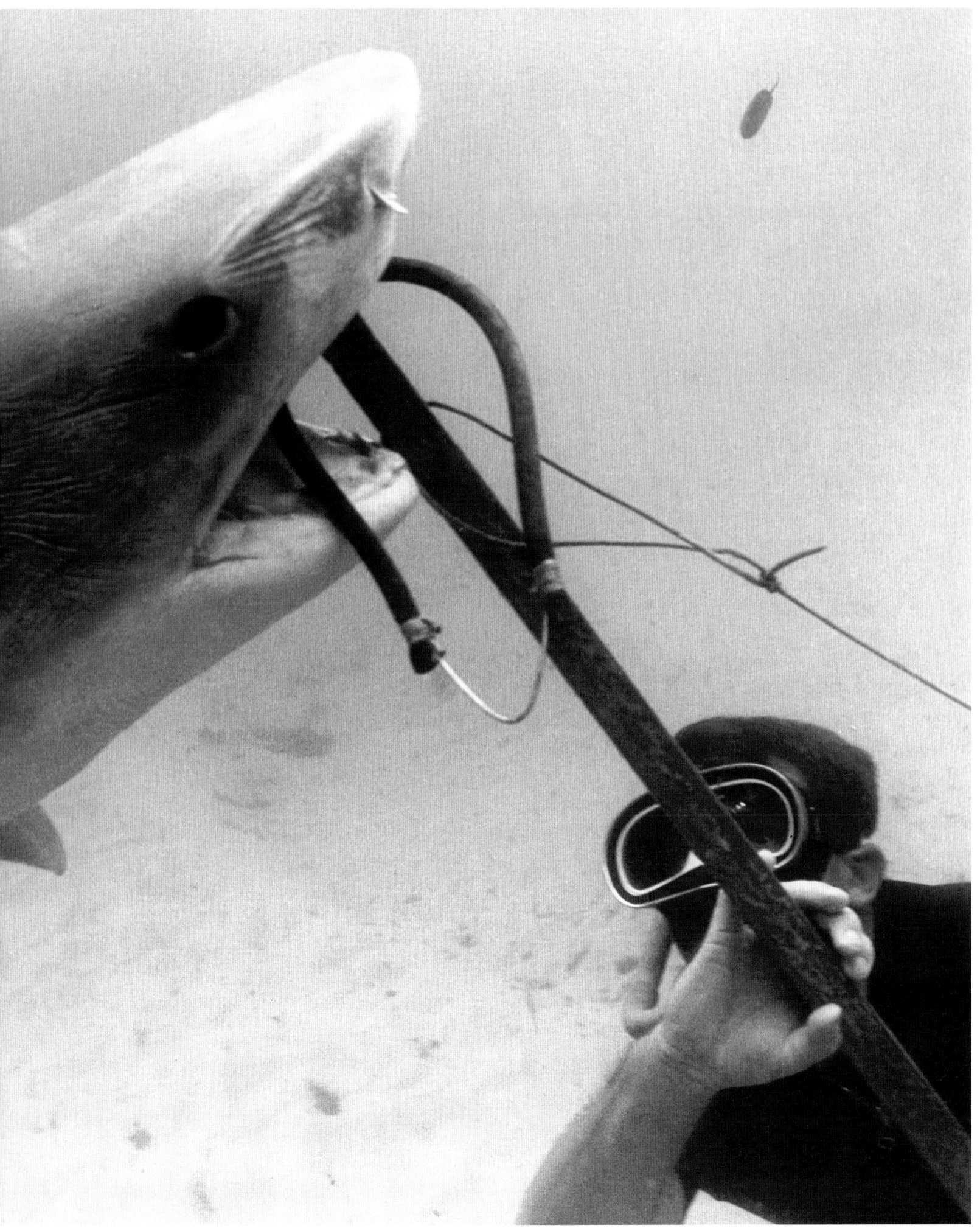

Far left: green turtle hatchlings are easy prey for a whaler shark. Left: with trophies I won at the 1958 Australian Spearfishing Championships.

When the other teams arrived from Sydney and Melbourne, they laughed at our primitive equipment, especially our inner-tube and copper-band masks. During that first decade we didn't even have snorkels, which we regarded as just some newfangled contraption. Once we tried them we couldn't live without them, but back then we relied on the skills we had picked up from long hours of trial and error. Diving every day as we did, we could hold our breath underwater for a couple of minutes at a time and, with no wetsuits, we were used to staying out in just about any conditions.

By the end of the championships, no-one was laughing at us any more. We won every event and I took out the Australian junior title. That was how it started for me. Over the next 10 years, I won six Australian titles for spearfishing and one for scuba, and diving went from being my hobby to my obsession.

Back in 1958, no-one could envisage making a good living as a diver, me included. All I knew was that there was a world full of exotic diving sites out there and teaching school in Colleville and marrying Miss Gold Coast wasn't going to get me to them. If I needed any convincing, it came from Des Conaghan, a keen fisherman from Coolangatta whom I had met around the traps. He had become my friend and mentor. I was drawn to him at first because he knew so much about fishing, but I soon found he was knowledgeable about a lot of things. He was much older than me, well-educated, highly intelligent and I think he saw in me a lot of himself at the same age. Like me, Des had always dreamed of visiting exciting locations around the world, but he had never got there. Instead he married young, had six children and did his travelling through the pages of books. He pleaded with me to take off overseas. I think he wanted to experience

the places he had always dreamed about through my eyes. I had great respect for him and wanted to follow his advice, but at the same time I felt I just couldn't desert Janie.

It was my youngest sister, Evelyn, whom we all called "Tiny", who came to my rescue. One day Janie was complaining to her that I was always out spearfishing and not being as attentive as she felt I should be. Tiny came up with a suggestion I will always be thankful for. "Look," she said. "I know how much Ben loves you, but he needs to be taught a lesson. Why don't you break off the engagement and, when Ben realises what he is missing out on, he'll soon come crawling back."

Which is exactly what happened – the first part of the plan anyway.

A four-metre tiger shark feeds on a marlin (photo by Lynn Cropp). Above, the triumphant team from Tweed Heads with spearfishing spoils at the 1959 championships (I'm at left).

I approach a giant groper surrounded by a host of pilot fish (photo by Lynn Cropp). Right: I was Australia's sole representative at the World Spearfishing Titles in Malta in 1959.

Janie handed me back the engagement ring, I got what I could for it and booked a one-way passage to England with 150 pounds to my name. I wouldn't be back for two years. Janie and I still speak on the phone from time to time. We've remained friendly and, with the passing of the years, I think she came to understand the relief I felt as I stood on the deck of that ship watching the shoreline of Australia dissolve into the distance.

My routine in England was pretty simple. I got jobs as a relief schoolteacher and headed off diving as soon as I could save enough money for a ticket. When the dough ran out, I'd head back to London and take another relief job.

One of my first stops was Malta for the 1959 World Spearfishing Championships. Like the Australian titles, this was a team event, but the Australian association was unable to send a three-man team, so I was it. I finished ninth out of more than 40 three-man teams.

When winter hit England, like any self-respecting Australian I went looking for the sun, ending up in the Canary Islands where I linked up with a couple of other divers. Every day we would spear fish and sell them to local shops and hotels to finance our accommodation and living costs. One day I saw a large yacht on its way to the West Indies and talked my way onboard as a deckhand. I jumped ship in San Juan, Puerto Rica, and got a job as a dive instructor at the Caribe Hilton hotel, saving enough for a cheap ticket to New York.

My plan was to get a boat from there to London, where I had some money waiting for me, and then to go to Sicily for the 1960 world spearfishing titles. In New York, the only ticket I could buy took every cent I had and, with a day or two to fill before sailing, I was dead broke. I went to the Australian Consulate and was ushered into the office of the Consul-General. I explained that I was an Australian champion diver trying to join the national team in Sicily. He handed me $30, recording the debt in my passport, and gave me some advice, which I took very seriously. "Go home, young man," he said. "Your country needs you." I'll never forget it. It was another of those turning points for me. I had been away from home a long time, and he was right. It was time to stop drifting around the world and to do something positive with my life.

When I got back to London after the world championships, I saw an advertisement calling for a shipboard chaperone to accompany a group of teenagers to Australia as part of the Outward Bound programme. I had an interview, played up the schoolteacher-son-of-a-Methodist-minister angle, got the job and was handed a free ticket home.

There on the dock in Sydney to welcome me back was Tiny, my little sister who had helped me escape from the Gold Coast. It was not quite the homecoming of the triumphant world traveller I had envisaged — I had to ask her to lend me the train fare to Tweed Heads — but I was not concerned because, by then, I had an idea; a way to keep diving, and make money doing it.

A creature of the deep
in the shallows:
eye to eye with a four-
metre tiger shark.

In the frame

IN 1961, the field of what would later become known as "nature films" was a market yet to be tapped. My hero, Hans Hass, had retired from underwater filming, and Jacques Cousteau had yet to become world-famous through his television series. Five years after its introduction into Australia, the popularity of television was going through the roof. Something told me Australian audiences would be drawn to films depicting the wonders of their own waters. After all, people like my mentor, Des Conaghan, would question me for hours about what I had seen and done at diving spots around the world. What better way to share my experiences than to capture them on film?

There was only one small hitch. I didn't have a movie camera, nor did I have the slightest idea how to use one. It was not as if I hadn't tried my hand at underwater photography. In the mid-1950s, just for a bit of fun, I made a watertight container for my little German-made still camera and took some shots underwater, including one of a shark, which I sold to a newspaper. It was my first-ever published photograph. The only problem was that the newspaper printed it upside down and, because the shark didn't look scary enough, the editor had an artist draw in an eye and some teeth.

Soon after returning home to Tweed Heads, I travelled to Phillip Island, south of Melbourne, and won the 1961 Australian spearfishing title. Nice as it was to add to my collection of trophies, it was more important to get together with the spearfishing community and ask some questions about underwater photographers. The name I heard over and over was Ron Taylor. Everyone I spoke to was of the same opinion: Ron was the best underwater cameraman in the country – not that there were too many others. He was a photo-engraver by profession but, like me, he had been bitten by the diving bug. Being in the business, it was a natural progression for him to try his hand at

Catch of the day: a tiger shark captured at Murray Island in the Torres Strait.

filming underwater and he had put together some footage, which he would show to fellow divers. There was no money involved at that time, it was just a hobby he could share with growing numbers of diving enthusiasts.

Two events combined in the late 1950s and early 1960s to trigger huge interest in diving. The first was the development of scuba (Self Contained Underwater Breathing Apparatus). Needless to say, the ability to strap on a tank and remain underwater for long periods revolutionised diving. The sport had come a long way in a short time from the days of homemade masks and spears. Jacques Cousteau and Emile Gagnon designed and tested the first aqualung in 1943 and their 1952 book *Silent World* launched the recreational scuba industry.

My first attempt at scuba could easily have been my last attempt at anything. In 1953 an Australian-made scuba called Porpoise came on the market, and I was given one to try out. The tank differed from most others in that it was upside down, and had two knobs at the bottom – one to turn on the air in the main tank and the other to turn on the reserve tank. I dived down about 10 metres and, when my air ran low, reached back with my left hand and managed to turn the air off instead of switching the reserve on. This left me with what we call a "free ascent" to the surface. The belief that the bends is the main killer of divers is a fallacy. More divers die from suffering an air embolism during a free ascent than from anything else. Basically, as the pressure lessens closer to the surface, the air in the lungs expands and they rupture. Luckily I was schooled enough to breathe out as I ascended, but it was a scary experience for a first dive nonetheless.

The other enormous shot in the arm for scuba diving around the world was the television series *Sea Hunt*, which starred Lloyd Bridges. It began in 1959 and was a smash hit everywhere it was shown. Unlike other diving footage just starting to be shown on film, *Sea Hunt* was a scripted series combining dramatic storylines with underwater scenes. A secret world enjoyed until then by just a few enthusiasts was suddenly being shared with millions.

It was during this exciting period in scuba history that I tracked down Ron Taylor. He had been filming on the Great Barrier Reef and we met at

Art and nature merge in this dramatic red gorgonia coral.

Tweed Heads on his way back to Sydney. My pitch was simple. "You're a cameraman, I'm a diver," I told him. "I'll dive, you film me." Ron agreed and I followed him back to Sydney.

Even though I was new to the film business, I was cluey enough to realise that if I were to get anywhere I would have to start in Sydney where the money and the media were. Ron and I also knew that we had to make a big splash with our first film. We needed a "hook" that would attract plenty of publicity and lure a big audience. We weren't trying to make art films, we wanted mass appeal, and I discovered I had a natural instinct for what people wanted to see and a flair for self-promotion.

As it would turn out, people around the world were fascinated by sharks. These creatures were dangerous yet beautiful, the ultimate killing machine. Or that's how they were viewed back then. Ron and I worked on a simple shooting script. I would dive down and kill as many sharks as I could, and he would film me doing it. We took the concept to Channel Nine and they loved it, offering us $1,500 for the footage. They would edit it and add a commentary.

Today, in these ecologically enlightened times, such a premise seems bloodthirsty and cruel, but people have to judge us in line with the attitudes that prevailed. In 1960 people were scared stiff of sharks, mainly because they were so ignorant about them. I like to think the films I made over the years educated people about sharks and other sea creatures, and helped change public attitudes towards them. Not that it happened straight away. From the time Ron and I made our first film, 1962's *Shark Hunters*, to some four years later when I vowed never to kill another shark, I killed hundreds and didn't receive so much as one note of criticism. The feeling then was that "the only good shark is a dead shark" and, as long as the TV networks wanted to buy film of me doing the killing, I was happy to oblige. Today it might seem abhorrent; back then it was just the way things were.

Shark Hunters was a runaway success in Australia and internationally. Ron and I didn't make a lot of money from it, but it established our

*The undersea world
captivated me. What
started as a hobby
became an obsession
and then a career.*

reputations among the world's top underwater filmmakers.

The following year, despite a good working relationship, Ron and I decided to end our partnership and go our separate ways. It was hard enough in those days to make money from underwater films without splitting the profits two ways. Ron headed back to the Barrier Reef and I stuck to filming sharks.

Once again I had the problem of not being a cameraman. Ron had never let me touch his camera, but I had spent plenty of time watching the way he worked and was confident I could handle the twin roles of diver and cameraman. The Commonwealth Bank failed to share my optimism and rejected my loan application. The ANZ Bank had more faith and I was able to buy a 16-millimetre underwater camera.

Filming came easily to me. I didn't have enough money to do any test shots, so I just went out, got in the water and filmed. I took the footage to Channel Seven and sold it for $1,000 and the cost of post-production. *Shark Safari*, my first film, was a huge ratings winner and, six months later, I was named World Underwater Photographer of the Year at the 7th International Underwater Film Festival in Santa Monica, California. Photographers and filmmakers from the US, Japan, Canada and Europe were competing, and when my film was shown the crowd applauded and some of the women in the audience screamed with each shark kill. Being the first Australian to win the main award was a major honour, but of greater significance to me were the names of previous winners. To be spoken of in the same breath as Jacques Cousteau and my hero Hans Hass was something I'll never forget.

As promotion for the film and with an eye to a long partnership, Channel Seven paid for me to fly to the US to receive my award and appear on TV talk shows. With the confidence that comes only from a total lack of insight into the enormity of the task, I decided that while I was there I'd just pop over to New York and sell the film to a big US network. No Australian filmmaker had ever sold a programme to the US, but I didn't give that a second thought. At the film festival, I asked around and

The days when I was a shark hunter … I speared this grey nurse shark in 1963.

Young lemon sharks photographed at the back of my boat. We would hang dead fish in the water until the sharks picked up the scent, and then film them eating. Lemon sharks can grow to about 3.5 metres and have been involved in several attacks on humans.

someone gave me the name of a guy at NBC who was in charge of a weekly series hosted by a former basketball star called Bud Palmer. His was the only name I had.

I arrived in New York and rang the number straight away. It was 5.30 on a Friday afternoon, the worst possible time to try to do business in New York City. By some miracle, the producer answered his own phone. I told him who I was and that I had a film to sell, and he told me to get in a cab and come straight around to his office. I walked in, sat down and told him about *Shark Safari*. He said, "Yeah, I'll buy it. What else have you got?" I told him about *Shark Hunters* and also about *Sea Snakes*, which was still on the drawing board. "Yeah," he said. "I'll buy them, too."

By Monday morning I had the signed contracts in my hand and was thinking, "Gee, this film business is easy." As the years went by, the selling business got more and more difficult. I went on dealing with that same producer, but he was never such a pushover again. Eventually I asked him: "What's the story? The first day we met, you bought everything I had and more. How come it was so easy then and it's so hard now?"

"Well, Ben," he said. "It was like this. That afternoon we were sitting around my desk having a meeting and we got the word that three films we'd ordered had dropped off the schedule. I'd just said, 'Where the hell are we going to get three more films in a hurry?' when the phone rang and it was you."

Luck like that doesn't happen too often in the film industry, but it happened for me that day, and set me on a roll which has lasted more than 40 years.

Left, creatures of the deep, including a butterfly fish, a potato cod and a diver (Photo by Lynn Cropp). Right, a marine iguana in the Galapagos Islands.

Shark hunter

Left: Wally Gibbons with a 4m tiger shark he killed with a .303 explosive head on a speargun. Above: my first wife, Van, killed this 2.2m whaler shark with a 12-gauge shotgun off Tweed Heads, NSW.

THE STRANGE thing about all this shark-hunting business is that, until I climbed into the water with Ron Taylor and he switched on his camera to start our first film, I had never killed a shark. The whole purpose of me becoming a shark hunter was to make a film and the success of that film and those that followed earned me a reputation I have never been able to shake.

Until Ron gave me the thumbs-up and I speared my first shark, I had taken an interest in sharks but always made sure not to get too close to the most feared and misunderstood creatures of the sea.

Like all spearfishermen around Tweed Heads, I had seen plenty of sharks and for some reason I had taken an almost scientific interest in

them. Every spearfisherman is aware of the dangers of spearing a fish when a shark is about. Blood in the water is like a switch that can turn a calm shark into a killing machine, and the spearfisherman who doesn't have an eye open for sharks is a fool. Each time I had an encounter with a shark I would note it down in what I called my "shark log". Some people like bird-watching, I became a shark watcher. Many of the sharks I encountered were great whites, the most dangerous species to be found in cooler waters, attracted by the fish I was spearing. I found that great whites were not aggressive, but I would never trust them and always made sure I knew where they were. As I would find with tiger sharks, the warm-water equivalent of the great white, they would circle slowly in the distance just in the periphery of my vision, always watching what I was doing. It was as if they were summing me up, which, needless to say, could be unnerving. Still, I liked to think I was always in control of the situation. It was only when I saw the film *Jaws* in 1974 that I changed my opinion about the great white. It put the fear into me, as it did for millions. After *Jaws*, anyone filming a great white did so from the safety of a cage.

When Ron Taylor and I started planning our first film we decided the species of shark I should target would be the grey nurse. In a way we were taking advantage of public ignorance. A number of attacks around Sydney Harbour had made people petrified of sharks. One of the most horrible and highly publicised had occurred on Australia Day 1963, just as our film was being completed. A young actress, Marcia Hathaway, was attacked while wading in shallow water at isolated Sugarloaf Bay near Castlecrag on the North Shore. She was rushed by speedboat to the nearest inlet, Mowbray Point, and a waiting ambulance but the ambulance was unable to get back up the steep dirt access track. A group of men got behind and pushed, but the clutch burned out, and the injured woman had to be carried by stretcher to a second ambulance at the top of the hill. She died before reaching hospital.

It was a horrific chain of events, made all the more shocking because the graphic images were captured by press photographers and TV cameramen and shown often over the next few days.

Taiwanese divers leap into
the water to kill giant clams.
Photo by Lynn Cropp.

As with most attacks in Sydney Harbour, the public assumed the killer was a grey nurse shark. In fact it was a bronze whaler, but as with attacks by great whites, the grey nurse copped the blame in the media. This notoriety, plus the fact that the grey nurse is easy to hunt, made it a perfect quarry for our purposes.

Originally I killed sharks under the banner of scientific research in a quest for an effective shark repellant. In the first *Shark Hunters* film, I am shown experimenting on whaler sharks with different methods of ridding the waters of this so-called dangerous menace. We developed a syringe on the end of a spear, which injected the whaler shark with various strengths of strychnine-nitrate. If a certain amount didn't kill the shark in the required time, we would top up the dose.

Unfortunately, the success of the film and my subsequent shark documentaries initiated the sport of shark-hunting. The more people saw, the less they were interested in research or scientific methods of killing sharks. They just wanted to see sharks killed, as spectacularly and as often as possible.

At first I used a barbed spear, similar to the one my friend Barry and I had designed as teenagers for the local blacksmith at Lennox Head. The point of this had been so that a speared fish could not get away. The problem with using this sort of spear on sharks was that if they were not killed instantly, the last thing you wanted was a thrashing shark caught on the end of your spear. Ever tried to subdue a wounded shark? There are easier things to do. What we came up with was the killer spear, which is just a spear without a barb. If the spear killed the shark, well and good. If not,

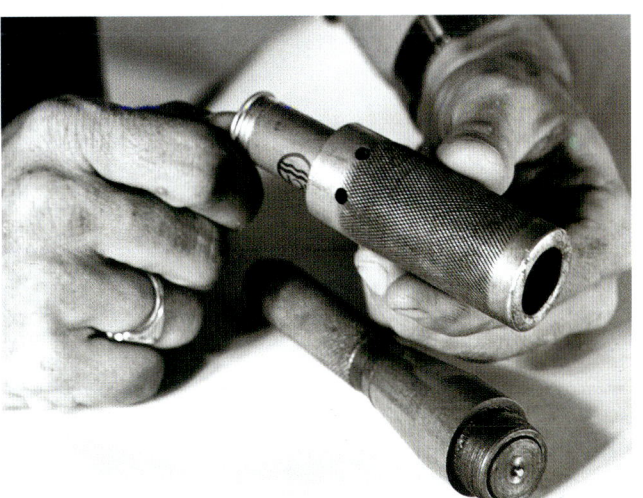

Jaws of death: a white tip reef shark dines out with friends. To kill sharks, we used an underwater shotgun with a 12-gauge cartridge. The other section shows the moveable firing pin.

the shark could swim away and lick its wounds and, with a hole in its side, it would take little interest in the diver. That was the theory anyway. It was a calculated risk I took often for the sake of the film.

Next we came up with a 12-gauge shotgun cartridge on the end of a hand spear, which was particularly effective on the slow-moving grey nurse. Later a version was developed with a .303 shell, which could be used on a speargun and fired from further away when hunting the faster bronze whalers or tiger sharks.

The introduction of explosive spearheads made a huge difference, not just for me but for any diver who wanted to hunt sharks – and plenty did. As my films were shown, every macho diver suddenly wanted to be a shark hunter and the explosive heads made the "sport" a lot easier and safer. One day while filming *Shark Safari* we killed 22 or 23 sharks, which I couldn't have done using the old methods. As well as killing sharks, I would try to find schools and swim among them, making for spectacular footage. The problem, of course, was what to do about the sharks you didn't kill. I might swim in a school of 20 sharks and poison one, but there were still 19 to contend with. Using an explosive head, this was no longer an issue because the explosion that killed one shark would frighten off the others.

I was a shark hunter for about four years before I began to have second thoughts about what I was doing. It might seem obvious today, but back then the idea that sharks were creatures that didn't deserve to die for sport was revolutionary. After all, this was a time in which dolphins were killed for fishing bait in NSW, and giant marlins were caught, killed, weighed and simply thrown on garbage tips.

Five years after I killed my last shark, I was invited to Japan to give a series of talks. When the plane landed, the tarmac was seething with reporters. The Australian Davis Cup team who were on board started putting on their ties and team jackets because they, like me, assumed the press was there to meet them. When we walked off the plane, it turned out the media was there to interview the great shark hunter. I wanted to say, "I don't do that any more", but I realised then, as I do now, that it is a reputation I will never leave behind. I guess it was a price I had to pay – a progression towards what would come next in my life.

Solomon Islander Harry, a shark caller, paddles out to meet the tiger shark that answered his call. Photo by Lynn Cropp.

The Shark That Changed My Life

I T WAS THE BIGGEST shark I had ever seen, which is hardly surprising because it was one of the biggest sharks anyone had ever seen.

It was in February 1965, and a week earlier the body of a monster whale shark had been washed up on a beach in Sydney's south. It created a huge stir with hundreds of people driving from all over the city to see it, have their photos taken standing alongside it and even to cut pieces from it as souvenirs or to feed to the cat.

A few days later I received a call from a good friend, George Meyer, who told me he had just seen a gigantic shark while diving near Montague Island off the NSW south coast. Realising it must have something to do with the whale shark washed up on the south Sydney beach, I told George I would be right down to see if we could find it. The chances of finding a specific shark in a designated spot are pretty slim, but George and I jumped in my little boat, which was a 14-foot fibreglass runabout, and headed out. By sheer chance, after a one-day search we found it. Sure enough it was a whale shark, more than 10 metres long. It was enormous, so big that it was hard to work out just how long it was. Up until that time the biggest shark I had ever seen was a five-metre tiger shark, but this made that seem like a tadpole. It was like the difference between a Mini Minor and a Mack truck. With every metre of length, there was a corresponding amount of bulk, giving the impression that this shark was four or five times larger than anything anyone had ever seen before.

When we came across it, George and I dived down and when I saw it up close I couldn't help but swear to myself. Though I knew that whale

A gentle giant: with son Adam, I'm filming a huge whale shark off Ningaloo Reef in WA (photo by Lynn Cropp). It's exhilarating to come face to face with a 10m shark, its 1.5m jaws open to feed as it glides post.

Friend George Meyer rides on the back of the monster whale shark, the biggest shark I ever saw. The day I spent filming it at Montague Island, NSW, in 1965 gave me the scoop of my life – and a new direction.

sharks, the largest members of the shark family, eat plankton and small fish rather than flesh, and are harmless, it was impossible not to have doubts because of its huge mouth. The mouth was so large it could have swallowed me whole without even noticing.

Pretty soon any reservations I had were gone. The shark might have been huge, but it was also friendly and very curious about us. When we spotted it, a number of other sharks and kingfish were swimming alongside, but eventually they swam off as the big shark kept coming back to look at us.

That shark gave us the most amazing experience of our lives. We filmed for an entire day. The water was clear, the conditions perfect, so I could use a slow film with the aperture wide open. No-one had ever filmed such a large shark. Hans Hass had once come across a giant whale shark unexpectedly, but he had a telephoto lens on his camera and no time to change it. The shark was so big that he had to stay a long distance away to get it all in shot, which ruined the effect. He also had only black-and-white film, while I was shooting colour. We were using 100-foot rolls of film, so whenever I ran out, I would have to swim back to the surface, reload and dive back down as fast as I could. When you consider that my boat was less than a third the size of the shark, you can understand my excitement.

That monster shark was the biggest scoop of my career, before or since. I sold the good clear still pictures from the footage around the world. Compared with the digital equipment now available, that old 16-millimetre Kodachrome film seems like something from the dark ages, yet the images were very good and they ended up being seen by millions. The Sydney *Sun* newspaper splashed a huge photo all over the front page and filled pages two and three as well. The story in *National Geographic* included a three-page fold-out, which showed the shark in all its glory. An English paper ran a teaser on the front page that read simply: "You've never seen anything like this before".

What made the pictures so stunning was the fact that George and I were able to go right up next to the shark and show its size. Unless you have a point of reference it is impossible to get a concept of size, and George provided that point of reference as I filmed him playing with the shark. The only time the shark showed any sense of uncertainty was at the

Adam (left) and I swim with a giant whale shark we encountered off Ningaloo Reef (photo by Lynn Cropp).

very beginning, when George grabbed its tail, hoping to be towed along. With one sharp sweep, it flicked him off as if he were an annoying bug. But as the shark became used to us it allowed us to get as close and personal as we liked.

It was incredible. We rode its back as if it were a giant seahorse. Its mouth alone was two metres wide – we could have swum down its throat sideways without touching the sides.

At the time I had just completed a film about taming marine creatures and was due to leave for the US to market it, but I was not satisfied with what I had. I felt the film lacked the punch of my previous movies and cancelled my trip in the hope of finding a hook to lure viewers. Incredibly, the day George rang with news of the whale shark was the day I would have been leaving for the US if I hadn't put the trip on hold. I didn't have to be Cecil B de Mille to realise the whale shark gave me the hook I needed, and then some. I quickly recut my film, renamed it Whale of a Shark and had another hit on my hands. That shark gave my career a huge boost, but it did a lot more than that. It changed my outlook on sharks forever. Even though I had created the shark-hunting industry and gained notoriety as its best-known practitioner, I was having second thoughts. What I did on screen might have looked dangerous but in fact I was extremely careful in everything I did and the odds were very much in my favour. With my killer spears and explosive heads, I had come to think of what I was doing not so much as hunting, but as slaughter. That day off Montague Island was the clincher. Being able to dive and play with the world's biggest shark, feeling totally at ease, had an enormous effect on me.

I would encounter whale sharks on several other occasions, most notably in 1972 when my second wife, Eva, friend Bob Dickson and I dived with a pair off Surfers Paradise beach for five hours, but nothing could compare with that gentle giant of seven years earlier. After that, I felt I couldn't kill another shark. I had been slaying sharks purely because people wanted to see them die. I never would again – not even for a million dollars.

A family friend:
the distinctive whale
shark off Ningaloo Reef.

Million-Dollar Maybe

CAN YOU IMAGINE being offered $1 million for a few minutes' work? More to the point, can you imagine turning it down, not once, but twice? That was the situation in which I found myself almost 10 years after I had vowed my shark-killing days were over.

By 1974 attitudes to sharks had mellowed. The public had become more educated and authorities had put into place measures, such as netting, which dramatically cut the chances of attacks on public beaches. And then along came *Jaws*. The best-selling book and smash-hit movie didn't just remind people about the dangers of sharks, it scared the heck out of them. Jaws wasn't just a film, it was a phenomenon, a part of popular culture. It was also an opportunity for me. In the decade since I had hung up my killer spear and 12-gauge shotgun shells, I had been making a whole new type of film. Gone were the shark-killing scenes and in their place was a genre that combined information and adventure. My new films proved more successful than the one-dimensional shark-hunting films, and the worldwide phenomenon that was *Jaws* created a mini-boom for my old stock. Channel 10 jumped on the *Jaws* bandwagon and commissioned me to put together a special on man-eaters, using my old footage. My old films were also suddenly in demand for re-runs around the world.

It provided a nice sideline to making new films and brought me back into the public eye, but there was one development, which even I couldn't have predicted.

Out of the blue I received a call from an American promoter. He wanted to stage a shark "fight to the death" live on TV and was offering me $1 million to take part. At first I thought it must have been a joke, but these were the days when specially staged live-to-air stunts were pulling enormous ratings. Events such as tennis player Bobby Riggs taking on Billie-Jean King; Muhammad

Idyll in the sun: Lynn, my third wife, among wheeling terns on a coral cay.

Ali fighting a Japanese wrestler and Evel Knievel attempting to jump a motorbike over the Grand Canyon were huge news. The promoter assured me he was very serious and it turned out a US television network was right behind him. He had finance in place, and Evel Knievel and Muhammad Ali were signed up as celebrity judges. It was going to be a Hollywood-style production with huge coverage around the world.

I told the promoter I wasn't interested. "I'm an ex-shark hunter," I said. "I don't do that any more." A few days later he was back on the phone pleading, and again I turned him down.

When he rang a third time, I have to admit I was wavering. The whole thing was starting to get a lot of publicity and my friends were calling and asking if I was out of my mind. "A million dollars to kill one shark?" they said, "Why not? You've killed hundreds of sharks in the past, what's one more dead shark in the grand scheme of things?" The more they said it, the more it seemed to make sense. There was the money and there was also the publicity. I would become a household name around the world and financially secure for life. But on the other side of the coin, I had made a decision 10 years earlier and going back on it didn't sit well.

Finally, with plenty of misgivings, I said yes – and that's when all hell broke loose. If I ever had any doubts that public opinion about shark-killing had changed, they were soon put to rest. The outcry was amazing. Irate people wrote letters to newspapers, the RSPCA came out against me. There was even an editorial in the *Wall St Journal*.

At one stage so many reporters were camped in front of my house (I was living at Pardise Waters, Surfers Paradise) that I jumped on my boat and headed out to sea. The general consensus was that, as the person who had been at the forefront of changing public opinion about sharks, I was being hypocritical by agreeing to kill one for money.

Even my mother rang and said, "Do you really want to do this, Ben?" That hurt. When your own mother joins the other side, you've got to ask yourself what's going on.

Still, I had agreed, and plans were pushing ahead. I had a back-up

Small-eyed and docile, a tawny shark manoeuvres with its entourage of pilot fish.

diver, a good spearfisherman named Wally Gibbons, and the two of us sat down to map our strategy for this so-called "contest". The rules were that Wally and I could pick any weapon we wanted. Our opponent was a great white, so with little hesitation we chose a hand-spear loaded with a 12-gauge shotgun shell.

We figured the fight would last five minutes before the shark was dead which, given it was supposed to be a one-hour programme, raised some technical problems, but these were the least of my worries. It wasn't so much the criticism I was getting in the media which was preying on my mind, it was more personal: I had changed direction after that day with the whale shark at Montague Island and it was against my principles to turn back.

Finally, I knew I couldn't go through with it. I invented a story about having a burst eardrum, which stopped me diving, and called Wally off the bench to take my place. I told the organisers I would still be there to support Wally, but I wouldn't take part in the actual "fight".

In the end, it was all academic. The promoter had a sudden heart attack and died, the shark lived and the TV network kept its million dollars. Call it karma.

Mangroves, home to box jellyfish (right) and shoals of baitfish (far right). Lynn photographed me filming this dangerous adult stinger. Note those long tentacles, each with millions of poisonous cells.

Tiger Tales

WHEN I CHANGED my attitude about hunting sharks I had to come up with another way to feature them in my films. Instead of filming myself and my companions killing sharks, I began filming us trying to avoid being killed by them. Sometimes that proved easier said than done, especially when I moved to the warmer tropical waters of northern Australia, habitat of the tiger shark.

One of my films was titled *Tiger Sharks – Legendary Thugs of the Sea*, and that sums them up perfectly. They are tough, mean and deadly, rated only behind the great white as a killer. My first encounter with a tiger shark taught me that this creature was different from any shark I had come across. Back in the days when I was a shark hunter, I had travelled to Queensland to do some filming and was on a commercial fishing boat. We were anchored at Swains Reef, east of Yeppoon, and one of the crew was filleting fish over the side to attract sharks. It didn't take long before a large tiger shark began feeding on the fish. The skipper and I hopped into a tinnie and headed towards it. Not having had anything to do with tigers before, I had serious reservations, but the skipper started egging me on. "Come on," he was saying, "you're the shark hunter, get in and kill him." With some reluctance, I slipped over the side and started swimming towards the shark, which then did something very unusual in my experience. As soon as it saw me, it left its food and headed straight towards me, something a grey nurse or even a great white had never done. I was used to being the hunter, and being the hunted is not a nice feeling. I headed straight back up and climbed into the boat as the shark cruised up alongside. It came so close that the skipper was able to reach down and touch its dorsal fin.

The year is 1964. Bela Csidei hauls aboard the 3m tiger shark he killed with a .303 explosive head.

I estimated that shark was five metres long and I never saw another one that large again. The largest were about four metres long, and what a difference a metre makes! A five-metre shark, with all its added bulk, appears twice as large as a four-metre shark. But over the years I found that tiger sharks are dangerous, no matter what their size.

The tiger shark is responsible for most attacks in tropical water. Its ferocity and the way it goes into a feeding frenzy at the taste of blood have earned it a fearsome reputation and offered me enormous filmmaking possibilities. They became my number-one subjects for the next 30 years. Close-up footage of tiger sharks ripping apart food with their awesome jaws earned me headlines and royalties around the world. Chasing that footage gave me some of the most frightening experiences in my career.

In the early days of filming tigers off Far North Queensland, I developed a routine. I would get the carcass of a giant marlin caught by game fishermen off Lizard Island, take it to nearby No Name Reef and tie it to the back of my boat. Then it was just a case of waiting. It might take half an hour, it might take an hour, but sooner or later there would be anything up to 10 tiger sharks feeding. I once saw 10 tigers dispatch a marlin that weighed about 450 kilos in 20 minutes. Obviously it was too dangerous to get right into the water when they were feeding, so I would simply lean over the back of the boat, with my head and arms in the water so that I could hold the camera and film. If, during this blind frenzy of feeding, it looked as if a shark were coming to take a bite at the camera, my companions on watch could warn me in time to pull up. Using this simple method, I could get the most spectacular vision of the sharks feeding, often as close as a metre from their jaws.

Shark-bait options changed when fishing practices changed. Most marlins caught were tagged and released. My next method was to go ashore and find a dead turtle. At the end of the nesting season in November, there are plenty of dead turtles on beaches for various reasons. They might have fallen off rocks, turned on their backs and dehydrated or just spent too much time laying their eggs in the hot sun and died of thirst. Other turtles might also have buried some accidentally as they dug down

A 4m tiger shark feeds on a huge dead marlin tied to the back of my boat.
Photo: Lynn Cropp.

to make their nests. As with the marlin, I would tie the turtle to the back of the boat and wait. It would take longer for the tigers to be attracted, sometimes a couple of hours, but eventually they would arrive.

One thing I will never forget is the sound of the sharks' teeth grating on the hard shell of the turtle. It was the most horrible noise and it gave me shivers down my spine.

Other times we would just anchor in the shallows at Batt Reef, 15 nautical miles off Port Douglas, and hang dead fish in the water until the sharks picked up the scent. It was an unreal sensation when they arrived. Tawny sharks, which are harmless, and lemon sharks, which are not, would usually show up first, followed by the tigers. The water would be so shallow and still that you could see perfectly everything happening under the surface. One time there were four tigers, three lemon sharks and four or five tawnys as well as a giant groper all feeding at the back of the boat, while at the front it all looked so peaceful you would swear you could go for a nice swim.

Spending so much time filming and observing tiger sharks, I learned a lot about them and came to the conclusion that it is unlikely that a tiger shark will just happen across a diver and take a bite. They like to take their time. They watch, get interested, get prepared and then attack. And once they start nothing will stop them. I believe that is why that first tiger came straight towards me. Usually a tiger shark would study a diver for a while before deciding whether to move in, but on that memorable occasion it had been eating the filleted fish we had thrown down and it saw me just as more of the same – a bigger morsel.

I also learned that they have a pecking order when feeding. They do not live as a pack, but the largest shark always takes precedence at meal times. The 10 tigers I saw tearing apart a marlin carcass did so one at a time. One would come in, rip off as much as its mouth could carry, then swim away allowing the next in line to take its place. The pack would continue to circle, eating in turn, but the largest shark would be allowed to jump the queue, coming in every third or fourth turn. Initially they can appear almost docile, but as they feed they become frenzied. Once when

A huge potato cod shows an interest in my underwater filming methods (photo by Lynn Cropp).

It was too dangerous to get right into the water when tiger sharks fed on the marlin tied to the boat. I would just lean over the back of the boat, with my head and arms in the water and film, sometimes just a metre away from those jaws.

a group of tigers were feeding on a marlin tied to my boat, one managed to get hooked up in the rope holding the marlin and was thrashing around trying to get free, but the others just kept on eating frantically, biting chunks out of one of their own in the process.

I've also seen tiger sharks attacking a whaler shark, which is not their usual diet, but when they get into feeding mode they will eat just about anything. The great white is similarly slow to attack, but once it makes up its mind it is unstoppable. If a shark attacks a swimmer it is usually because it thinks the swimmer is something else, perhaps a seal. It will not feast on a person in the manner of, say, a man-eating lion. It will come up and take a bite, almost experimentally to see what it tastes like, but that one bite can take off a limb and inflict fatal injuries.

My reputation as an expert on sharks was such that I was called as a witness at the coronial inquiry into the 1998 disappearance of American couple Tom and Eileen Lonergan, tourists left behind at St Crispin Reef after a commercial diving trip from Cairns. The dive boat skipper was acquitted of their manslaughter, and their fate inspired the 2004 feature film *Open Water*. I told the inquiry I believed tiger sharks had taken the Lonergans on the second day or night they were missing. There were times during my encounters with tigers that I was fortunate not to have met a similar fate.

How close is that!
Another angle as
the hungry tiger shark
surfaces to continue
making mincemeat of
the tethered marlin.

Close Encounters

THE HAIRIEST ENCOUNTER I've ever had with sharks didn't involve tigers or great whites, but whalers – not to be confused with whale sharks, those gentle giants. I was filming with Bob Dickson at Saumarez Reef in the Coral Sea, and we were in the water spearing coral trout. Bob had one on the end of his spear when two whalers arrived wanting a piece of the action. When a hungry shark has an eye on your catch it is a good policy not to argue. The whalers chewed up the trout and swam off, no questions asked. Then six more came in. They had seen the first pair feeding and wanted their share. Having missed out on the food, they saw us … and charged. One shark charging I can handle; six can be a problem. Bob and I swam backwards, kicking at the sharks with our flippers. We knew if the sharks got past the flippers we would be in big trouble. The sharks were hell-bent on biting us and if just one of them pierced a wetsuit and the blood started flowing, there would be no stopping the others. By textbook standards, they weren't big, maybe two metres, but with six of them coming at us, snapping their jaws, Bob and I weren't sticking around to measure them. We got to the boat and pulled ourselves to safety. I had kept the camera running during the entire attack and, when we played it back, we were surprised to find the whole encounter took exactly 15 seconds. It seemed like an eternity.

That experience always springs to mind when people ask me about the dangers of getting too close to sharks, but there have been others almost as scary, and all involved tiger sharks.

Unfortunately, when you have been doing something a long time, you tend to become a little blasé, even complacent. You cut a few corners and take some risks you wouldn't have considered when you were new to the job. It only takes a momentary lapse in concentration to remind you that

Feeding frenzy: a school of whaler sharks feeds on dark masses of sardines at Cape Cuvier in Western Australia.

Dead fish dangled
from my boat was
irresistible bait for
sharks. It was an
unreal sensation
when they arrived.
Tawny sharks, which
are harmless, and
lemon sharks (right),
which are not, would
usually show up
first, followed by
the inevitable tigers.

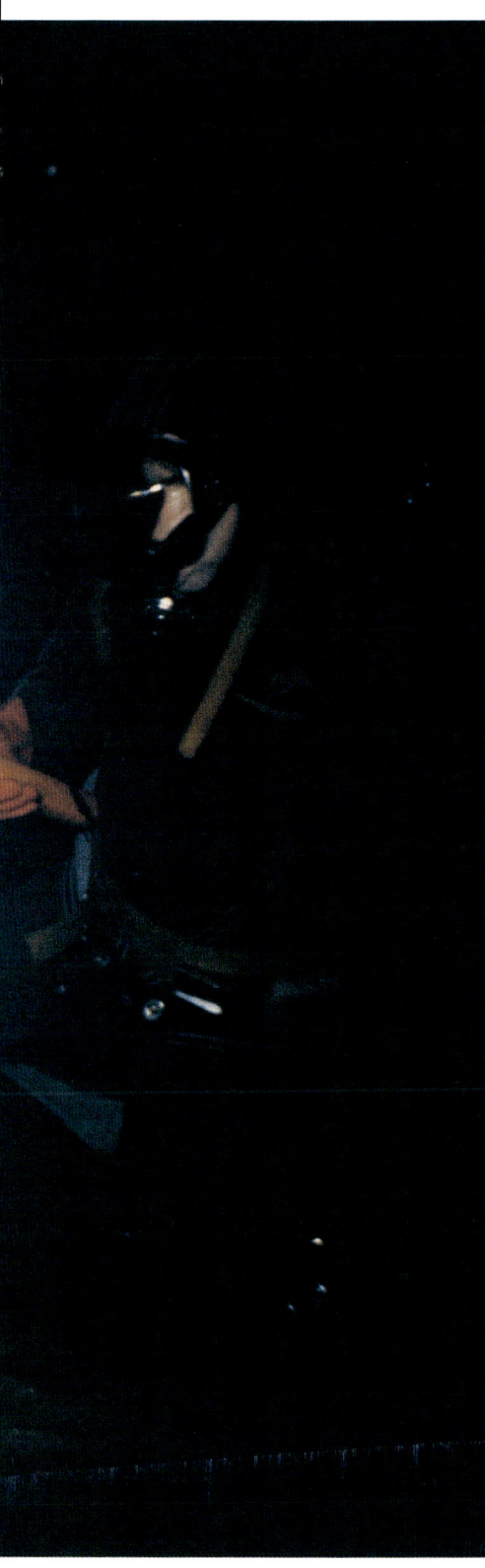

considering anything "routine" about sharks can be a fatal error.

In 2004 I headed out to do some filming at Batt Reef with my partner, Trina Fleischmann, a longtime family friend whom I had taught to dive and who had accompanied me on many trips, and journalist and ex-shark hunter John Harding. Just as I had done when I was a schoolboy at Tweed Heads, I always like to catch our meals when we are at sea, so the first thing we did after anchoring my boat *Freedom* was to go out to spear some fish in the shallow water. The three of us jumped in my dinghy, along with my silky terrier, Tuffy, and headed off. My dinghy is actually a 3.8-metre "rubber ducky" with a hollow PVC pontoon on each side housing an inflated inner tube.

As we searched for a good place to spear fish, we came across some Torres Strait Islanders harpooning from a tinnie. Thinking they might be hunting dugong, or sea cows, which is illegal in that area without a permit, we went over to investigate. "No dugongs," they told me, "just a turtle." Satisfied, we waved and kept going and ran straight into a tiger shark. Unbeknown to us, the shark had been attracted by the scent of the turtle's blood. Not knowing it was "in the zone" and desperate for food, I told John to follow the tiger while I filmed it. Once we got on the top of the tiger it came up, bumped the dinghy and disappeared. It was like a scene from *Jaws*. We were all looking around. "Where is it? Where has it gone?"

It wasn't long before we found out. With a "whoosh" of water and a snap of its jaws, the shark's head came out of the water as it bit the side of the dinghy – half a metre under Trina's backside. I wasn't too concerned at this point. I thought the shark would realise there was nothing tasty about a rubber ducky and would swim off, but its teeth had cut straight through the PVC pontoon into the inner tube and it was stuck fast. For five minutes that shark ripped, tore, rolled and shook its head frantically as it tried to get free. The water was so shallow it couldn't lift its teeth out of the fabric and, the more it tried, the more frenzied it became. With every twist of the shark's head, the inner tube deflated more and the dinghy listed towards it.

At first, my priority was to keep filming but, as I ran out of tape, the survival instinct took over. John kept snapping away with his digital camera as we all moved over to the other side of the dinghy. Well, nearly all of us. Tuffy decided he wanted a better view of the threshing machine in action below and put his front legs on the deflating pontoon so he could look over the side. John had to climb over and pull him back. The longer the shark

 *Diver Mike Pashkoff confronts a whaler shark at night.*

was stuck, the more worried we became that the dinghy would flip over. We yelled out to the group of Islanders, and they came towards us. "Stay close in case you have to pick us up," I shouted. Happily, it didn't come to that. Somehow the shark broke free and swam off. The dinghy was a bit wobbly but still seaworthy so we were able to limp back to the big boat.

Once there, we replaced the inner tube and stuffed a mat into the pontoon to cover the hole. It was still a bit wonky, but we had no choice but to go out again because we still hadn't caught anything to eat. Also, I believe when you have had a good scare it is best to hop right in again. It lessens the build-up of fear. It is a technique I have seen employed by native divers many times. When one has a close shave, the others will joke and tease him until he has a smile on his face, and then they will all go diving again. Trina wasn't doing much laughing when we got back from our close encounter. In fact, she was in shock, but she still came back out with us. We headed to one of my favourite fishing spots and what should be there but a tiger shark. John and I decided that one of us should spear while the other "rode shotgun". While I kept my eye on the shark, John speared a coral trout and it was then my turn to fish. I was about to jump in on a "bommie", which is a submerged coral outcrop, but found I would not be alone. Five tiger sharks were circling. Given that we were quite close to where the Islanders had speared their turtle, I had second thoughts.

"Let's get out of here," I said to John. "Let's go right over to the other side of the reef." We started up the engine and tottered off in our wounded dinghy. One of the tiger sharks followed us part of the way.

When we got to the other side of the reef, I slipped into the water. I was nervous. While we were at Batt Reef I counted 15 tiger sharks in water no more than two metres deep. Eventually we got back to the *Freedom* with plenty of fish for a good dinner, but that was one day I wished I'd brought along some canned tuna instead.

Here's the evidence of the tiger shark attack. With me in the partly deflated boat is a shocked Trina Fleischmann, arm around Tuffy in his lifejacket. Photo by John Harding.

Nasty Business

TIGER SHARKS were my major subjects for many years, but two other creatures I filmed also come under the heading of what I call "the nasties". I prefer to call them that rather than man-eaters, killers or predators for one simple reason. Who wants their kids to watch a show that sounds as if it will give them nightmares? Besides, one of the reasons I was so keen to make films about the nasties was so that people would learn more about them and, perhaps, with knowledge, feel safer.

The first was the sea snake, supposedly the most venomous of all snakes. In fact this is a reputation rather unfairly earned. It is true that sea snake venom is strong, but it is slow-acting and so there is time to seek treatment. Another bad rap the sea snake doesn't deserve is its reputation for aggression. Sea snakes are remarkably docile for most of the year. They also have poor eyesight, which makes it difficult for them to see quarry, let alone stalk it. In fact, if divers freeze when a sea snake approaches it will float around or slide over them without any problem. It is only during the mating season, around June, that the sea snake turns from Mr Magoo into Freddy (*Nightmare on Elm Street*) Krueger. If a diver so much as accidentally brushes a sea snake with a flipper during the mating period, there will be trouble. The snake will attack without apparent cause or warning. It makes for great action photography, but it doesn't do much for the blood pressure.

Photo-journalist Kenneth McLeish once asked me to help with a story on sea snakes that *National Geographic* had commissioned him to do. I took him out on my boat so we could take shots of the snakes going about their business, but the magazine wanted something more spectacular. The editors radioed Kenneth and told him what they had in mind. "Ben," he

An olive sea snake in aggressive mood. The largest I encountered were about two metres long.

told me afterwards. "We've got to get some shots of a snake attacking a diver." "Sure," I said, and we set off again, which pleased Kenneth enormously. I don't think he would have been quite so happy if he knew he was going to be the one attacked. When we had been out earlier, Kenneth had stressed that if either of us were attacked by a sea snake the first priority for his companion was to get the shot and then come to the rescue, which was fine by me. This time we dived down together and when I saw a nice quiet sea snake floating past minding its own business, I picked up a bêche-de-mer, a kind of sea cucumber, and hit the snake on the head. It went absolutely berserk and charged straight at Kenneth, and started biting at his wetsuit, once, twice, three times as I snapped away with my camera. When I had the shots, I moved in and pushed the snake away, then swam back to the boat with Kenneth. If I'd thought the snake was angry, it had nothing on Kenneth. He was livid.

"What were you doing?" he said. "Why did you do that? Why didn't you help me?"

I reminded him of his edict about taking the shot first, but he seemed to have forgotten about that. Still, he had his story and his photographs, and *National Geographic* was happy, which cheered him up no end.

As I continued to film and swim with sea snakes, I learned a lot more about them, often by trial and error. After being attacked several times, I realised there is an unmistakable warning sign that they are getting angry. Ignore the warning and they charge. Filming off Marion Reef, in the Coral Sea east of Mackay, I followed sea snakes around like an underwater paparazzo. Every time a snake moved I was there with my camera, which the snake would accept for a while, but if I got too close it would release bubbles from its nostrils. This was the sea snake's way of saying "back off" and, once I worked that out, it made life a lot easier for both of us.

The largest sea snakes I filmed were about 2.5 metres long, which is pretty much their maximum size. The average length is 1.5 metres. Their venom, which acts to immobilise their prey so they can eat it, is injected after the snake "mouths" the quarry to make sure it is edible. The routine is to grab, mouth, taste, then inject, which offers a few seconds to escape – a window of opportunity which the snakes' targets rarely get a chance to make the most of. It is an incredible sight to watch a sea snake feeding, the way it engulfs a paralysed fish head-first, even though the rest of the fish is much wider than the head.

From a diver's point of view, one thing to our advantage is that a sea snake's fangs are quite short, about five millimetres, the same thickness as

Perhaps the nastiest of what I call "the nasties": the blue box shape and trailing tentacles of a juvenile box jellyfish (above); and a pair of olive sea snakes mating. Each creature can pack a lethal punch.

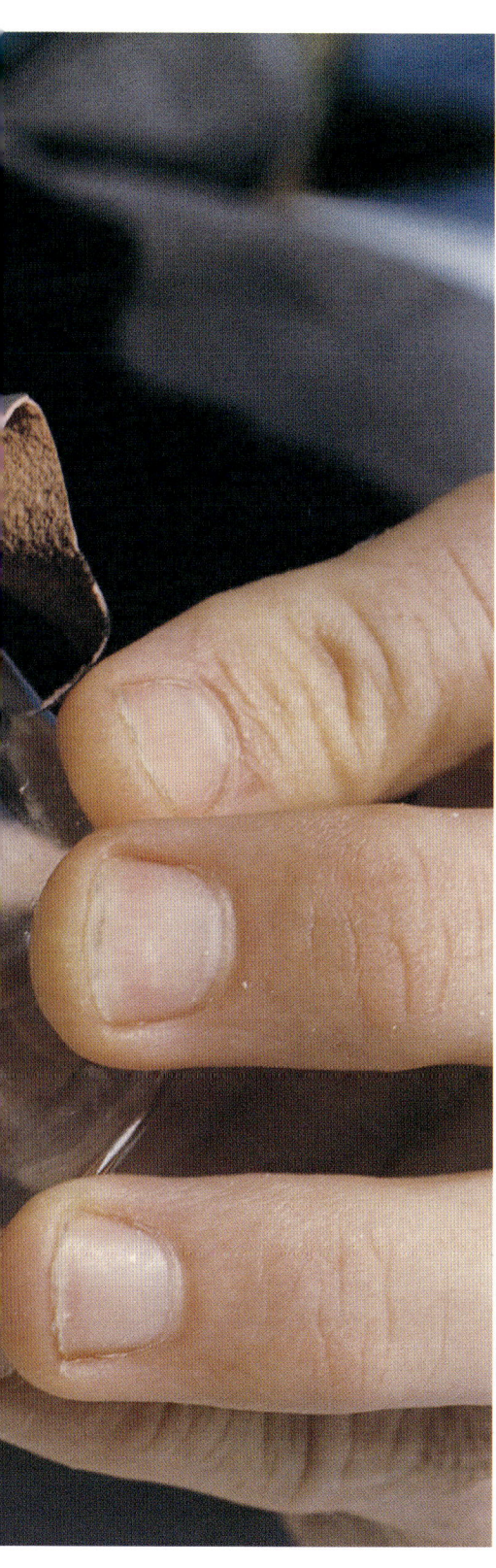

a wetsuit. Only very large snakes can pierce a suit and deliver their venom, which is why most fatalities inflicted by sea snakes have occurred on board fishing trawlers. Fishermen accidentally grab a snake while emptying their nets, are bitten and, being far from land, have little chance of getting treatment.

It was for that reason that I always wore gloves when handling the snakes in my films, but one of my offsiders had no such fears. Dr Glen Burns was a neighbour of mine in Port Douglas who had done a PhD on sea snakes. When he came out filming with me, he preferred to handle the snakes with his bare hands, believing it gave him more control. Maybe I should have taken his tip. In all the filming Glen and I did together, the only one of us who was ever attacked was me. Still, as long as we got the shot before he came to my rescue, I wasn't complaining.

The other "nasty" I filmed was a nasty in every sense of the word. The box jellyfish comes in two sizes, big and small. Both produce the most virulent poison known to man and, for its size, the smaller variety, the irukandji, is the most venomous creature of all. The size of a little fingernail, it can put you in intensive care with one touch of a tentacle.

As the name suggests, these jellyfish are box-like in shape. The small variety has just four tentacles, one on each corner of the box, the larger has groups of tentacles spreading from each corner.

Obviously the aim is to keep away from those tentacles, but, in order to test the strength of box jellyfish poison and assess first-aid treatments, I did the opposite. I guess we always wonder just how far we would go to do our jobs. In making my film on box jellyfish, I found out.

They had fascinated me for 20 years. They intrigued me, probably because so little is known about them and also because they were so prevalent near my Port Douglas home. I didn't have to travel far to film or study them. At certain times of the year, they would swim right past my jetty. All I had to do was lean over the side and turn on my camera.

While the tiny irukandji jellyfish is not so easy to find – I only ever saw one – its big cousin has a major effect on the lifestyle and the tourism industry of Far North Queensland. When I went to collect specimens for my studies, I saw literally hundreds of them. They are a lot more common

 *Milking a venomous olive sea snake. Usually docile, during the mating season these snakes may attack a diver without apparent cause or warning.*

The box jellyfish I'm holding measured 30cm across, which is the largest they grow. It was caught on Four Mile Beach, Port Douglas, a month after the official end of the stinger season.

than people think and can be found in large numbers close to shore from late November to the end of May, although I have seen them all year round except in July and August. Virtually transparent, up to 22 centimetres in size and therefore easy to step on or swim into, the box jellyfish lowers the standard of living in the Far North. Bathers must swim in enclosures or wear protective suits during "stinger season" and tourists are warned about the dangers of even wading in unfenced areas.

Yet for all that, the authorities are unwilling to seriously look into measures to control this dangerous threat to life and industry. The box jellyfish kills just as many people as sharks do in the Far North, but while control of sharks is a major priority, next to nothing is done to fight the jellyfish. The official line is, "It's there, it's dangerous, learn to live with it."

As always, I found making a film the perfect way to learn about my subject. It was my way of discovering and gaining new information I could never find between the covers of any textbook. I began filming box jellyfish in 1983 and over the next two summers I acquired a grudging admiration for them. They might look like an old plastic bag floating along on the tide, but they are very clever creatures, with strong survival instincts. It is rare to find a box jellyfish washed up on a beach except perhaps at the end of the spawning season. With four eyes, they manoeuvre their way around large objects, sneak up on small fish and, most amazingly of all, can sense impending bad weather or cyclones.

One day I was standing on my wharf and noticed large numbers of box jellyfish swimming upstream against the current, instead of heading out to sea. Like clockwork, 24 hours later we received a cyclone warning. Sure enough, the cyclone hit and next day the box jellyfish were back, swimming out to sea. I couldn't believe what I had seen, so I made a note to pay special attention during the next cyclone season. The same thing happened.

The most important discovery I made was that the box jellyfish is under threat from its own natural predators. The main one is the hawk's bill turtle. This turtle, which inhabits coastal areas, loves jellyfish and is obviously immune to the venom. Others include the batfish, butterfish, spinefoot and golden trevally. The blue swimmer crab is also skillful at reaching up and grabbing box jellyfish as they float by. While the turtle is protected, the other fish are not, despite their valuable contribution to controlling the jellyfish population.

To me, this was invaluable information. Here was a natural and inexpensive way to control a creature that is at best a pest and at worst a threat to life and the local economy. Of course, the authorities would not

*Incredible beauty
abounds in the waters
of the tropics and is
an endless source of
inspiration for all
marine photography.*

take my observations seriously without a proper scientific study for them to give an official stamp of approval. To this end, I applied for a government grant to finance a systematic scientific study. I would plan the study and oversee it, and qualified marine biologists would carry it out. At the time I was considered one of just three experts on the box jellyfish, but that was not good enough for the bureaucrats. I didn't have any official letters beside my name, so my years of research and firsthand experience counted for nothing. As I had so many times when confronted by a bureaucratic brick wall, I just kept doing things my way, camera in hand.

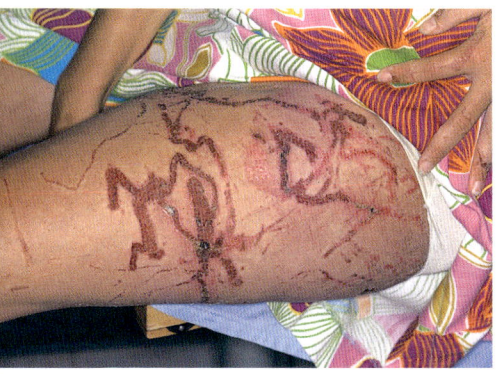

*Ouch! Above, Anne
Richards survived
a severe box jellyfish
sting, which left these
scars (photo from
Townsville Hospital).
Left, Michelle Mason
with the box jellyfish
she caught at Port
Bradshaw, NT.*

Not that I was in any fit state to hold a camera or anything else for that matter when I took the role of guinea pig to test the potency of the stingers' poison. It was painful, and it certainly made an impression. A few years ago I was in the North Queensland hinterland when I met a British girl who had just arrived as a tourist. She told me she was so excited to be there because she had seen a lot of films about the area on television in England and had always wanted to visit. I asked what films she had seen.

"There was one in particular," she said. "It was about this crazy guy who stung himself with box jellyfish venom."

I suppose she was right. I was crazy, but it was one of those things which I felt had to be done, and who could I possibly ask to do it? Besides, it made good television.

To make the film, I collected a number of box jellyfish and my then wife, Lynn, used them to sting me on one arm and then the other. We waited a minute or so until the poison took effect, and when I gave her the signal, she poured on the two so-called treatments, one kind on each arm. The recognised treatments at the time were methylated spirits and vinegar. The idea was that I could then state from personal experience which one worked better, meths or vinegar. My finding: neither.

These days we know that metho on a box jellyfish sting not only doesn't help, it makes the situation worse. When something comes into contact with a jellyfish tentacle it releases millions of poisonous capsules called nematocysts. Not all of them are active – until they are activated by methylated spirits, that is. Theoretically, vinegar has the opposite effect, but my experience was that it didn't stop the pain, which lasted at least 20 minutes. I also experimented with other possible treatments including an Aboriginal treatment made from the juice of the crinum lily. I would like to say that one worked, but I was never able to master the knack of getting the juice from the plant.

It was a painful and unpleasant experience, but not life-threatening. I knew from my research that any deaths from box jellyfish stings had been caused by a lot of tentacles and I wasn't going to put myself in that situation – which is not to say it didn't hurt. I liken it to being stung by a swarm of wasps. It reached its most painful when Lynn had run out of places to sting me. She had done my arms and chest and I cleverly suggested she rub a tentacle on my inner thigh, which might have been okay if she hadn't accidentally hit my groin. Now that hurt.

Still, I suffered for my art and it was captured on film. The worst sting I experienced was on a trip to northern Australia when I captured a very large adult box jellyfish and it slipped out of my hands and rolled up my arms, its tentacles releasing poison all the way. I think any professional cameraman will understand when I say I don't know what hurt more – the stinger or the fact that no-one got the shot. Either way, it wasn't fun, but if the occasional close call with a "nasty" is the price I have to pay to get across a message I believe is important, I figure it's worth it.

In an experiment to determine which first aid treatment (vinegar or methylated spirits) is better for jellyfish stings, Lynn subjects me to stings on both arms. (Result: Vinegar kills unfired stinging cells, but nothing kills the pain.) Right, filming a "stinger".

Poacher Turned Gamekeeper

BACK IN THE 1960s, if anyone had suggested that the Australian government would one day honour a shark hunter for conservation you'd think they were mad. Yet that is what happened to me in 1999. I owe my Order of Australia to the giant whale shark.

A film I made in 2004 showed that I had come full circle in both my attitudes to sharks and my actions. It was titled *The Vanishing Grey Nurse* and was aimed at protecting the last remnants of a species whose demise I had been a major contributor to 40 years earlier.

It wasn't just the shark-hunting craze that almost killed off the grey nurse. With commercial fishing and the numbers caught in shark nets off beaches, the species never had a chance to recover. By the time I made my film, the population had reached a critical level of perhaps just 500 along the Australian east coast. Marine scientists believed the grey nurse would be extinct in less than 10 years.

The film helped publicise the plight of the grey nurse. The shark was already a protected species in NSW waters and soon afterwards it became protected in Queensland as well, but that was only half the battle. Just as important as protecting the shark was protecting its habitat. The position was so critical that it was estimated that catching just two more females a year could drastically hasten its demise.

Eva, accomplished diver and beauty queen, swims with a giant manta ray at Lady Musgrove Island.

During its winter migration up the coast, the grey nurse is known to congregate in deep underwater gutters in certain spots off Southern Queensland. The sharks like such spots because they know they can find fish there. Fishermen feel the same way. I wrote to Queensland Premier Peter Beattie asking him to declare a grey nurse sanctuary. I told him I knew that fishermen hate to be told where they can and cannot fish. "I'm a fisherman myself," I wrote. "But if we don't want to see the extinction of this creature it must be protected."

It was one occasion when having a public profile helped. The Premier wrote back saying he was "chuffed" to hear from me, and he did indeed declare that sanctuary.

In ways such as this I have always been happy to lend my support to issues I believe in. I'm not a Greenie, although I believe Greenies have their place. I class myself as a conservationist. Sometimes, in order to conserve, we have to compromise. For that reason we need the excessive demands of the Greenies as a starting point from which we can reach middle ground. I have never joined any official organisation or movement because I feel I can do more good as an independent voice, and that independence allows me to say what I want to say through my films. We should never underestimate the importance of film, which educates as it entertains. It is the perfect medium to bring awareness to an issue without preaching. I remember the early days of diving when dolphins were being harpooned for bait. The public knew little about dolphins so nothing was said. Then producer Ivan Tors came along with his TV series, *Flipper*. The dolphin became an overnight star, the ocean's version of Rin Tin Tin or Skippy, and dolphins are now loved and protected around the world.

I helped bring about a seasonal closure of coral trout-fishing during the spawning season, and instigated the protection of potato cod at the Cod Hole, east of Lizard Island. Unfortunately, not all my campaigns were successful. Not everything in the ocean is as cute and loveable as Flipper or a potato cod. In the 1970s, I fought a losing battle to save the mangroves of the Gold Coast.

Death in bloody close-up: Lynn touches the frozen fin of a 4.6m great white shark.

I just couldn't make people understand that mangroves are a fish nursery, vital for every fish caught in the river or off the beaches. Even the local prawn fishermen refused to believe that the prawns they caught out at sea had grown up in the mangroves.

Mangroves were considered an eyesore; smelly mudflats ruining the view, and needless to say, the developers did nothing to debunk that impression. When developer Keith Williams built his Sea World theme park, he boasted that he was providing a public service by ridding the community of acres of ugly mangroves.

I never could save those mangroves, and it was the continued development of the Gold Coast that saw me move from Surfers Paradise to Port Douglas, north of Cairns, in 1980. Happily, my attempts to protect the mangroves near my new home were more successful, although not without problems.

Port Douglas was a quiet little village when I arrived, and then along came Mr Christopher Skase. He would later become known as one of Australia's greatest corporate rogues, but in the late 1980s he was at his peak. He owned the Channel Seven network, the Mirage hotel chain and was talking about buying MGM film studios in Hollywood. He also owned a large parcel of land at Port Douglas on which he built the magnificent Mirage resort, complete with 18-hole golf course. The locals accepted the development of their little paradise with regret but a certain inevitability. A jewel like Port Douglas couldn't stay secret forever, but when Christopher Skase announced he wanted to expand his golf course by another nine holes – and destroy all the mangroves along the south side of the inlet to do so – residents decided enough was enough. The townspeople called a public meeting to protest and they asked me, as an expert on mangroves, to be the main speaker.

There was just one problem. I was under contract to Channel Seven, and Skase was paying me $120,000 a year. I had been fighting to protect mangroves for more than a decade but, as I stepped up to the podium, I was a worried man. On one hand, I was passionate about saving the environment. On the other, I was passionate about feeding my family and continuing my lifestyle.

The entire town turned out to protest the planned development and the case of Port Douglas versus Christopher Skase made headlines nationwide. It was a fight we won. The Queensland government stepped in, the expansion of the golf course over Crown Land was stopped and that left only the issue of my professional future to clear up.

A vibrant and distinctively coloured trigger fish; these are usually found on coral reefs in tropical waters.

Where there's life, there's a food chain … Lynn took this photo of a crocodile swallowing a pig, and I took the photo of a grey nurse shark eating a blue groper.

The moment I heard Skase was back in town I went straight around to the Mirage to see him. I found him on the golf course and walked up to him, wondering just what his reaction would be.

"Hello, Chris," I said, not beating around the bush. "I'm sorry about having to block your expansion."

"That's okay, Ben," he said pleasantly. "I knew you'd have to."

A lot of people took an almost sadistic delight in Skase's subsequent downfall, disgrace and demise. Not me. I took him as I found him and, I have to say, even though he was in a position to be vindictive, he never did the wrong thing by me.

The PM's Last Letter

Like just about anyone who had ever dived there, I was passionate about protecting the Great Barrier Reef. The difference was that, thanks to my profile, I was able to get the ears of some powerful people.

In 1967 I approached Liberal Prime Minister Harold Holt, initiating a campaign to protect the reef from corporate interests. Many mining companies were licking their lips at the untapped riches lying beneath the reef, and local authorities were equally excited about the royalties such riches could bring. By 1968 the Queensland government had issued 16 permits to two oil companies to begin drilling across 80 percent of the reef.

Harold Holt was a fellow diver and spearfisherman, and I appealed to his instincts as a true man of the sea. A few weeks later, I received a letter from Canberra. It was from The Office of The Prime Minister and in it Holt said he agreed with my concerns and was pushing ahead with plans to have the reef declared a national park. "I have passed the matter on to one of my ministers for urgent action," he wrote.

The letter was unsigned. Just after dictating it, on December 17, 1967, Holt went bodysurfing in rough seas near his holiday house at Cheviot Beach, Portsea, in Victoria. He was never seen again. Mine was the last letter he wrote.

Many years later I was with former Prime Minister John Gorton on a boat off Raine Island south-east of Cape York and I told him about the letter and Holt's claim that he had passed the matter on to a minister. "Ben," Gorton said. "I was that minister. It cost me the Prime Ministership."

When Gorton became Prime Minister in 1968, he made Harold Holt's dream of protecting the reef a priority. In order to stop the Queensland government from allowing mining companies access to the reef, he placed it under the protection of the Commonwealth. The loss of potential revenue turned Queensland Premier Joh Bjelke-Petersen into Gorton's lifelong enemy. The mining lobby turned against him, and the other States, noting how he had ridden roughshod over Queensland, feared the same could happen to them in a similar situation. It all combined to add to the erosion of Gorton's support in the party room and, in 1971 when a party vote of no-confidence was deadlocked 33-all, Gorton used his casting ballot to vote himself out of office.

Before he went, he set the wheels in motion for the establishment in 1975 of the Great Barrier Reef Marine Park Authority, which is recognised as the most successful of its kind in the world. To me, it stands as a monument to the work done by John Gorton and the vision of Harold Holt.

 *A spectacular lion fish presides over a coral garden.*

Trash or Treasure

EVEN THOUGH I am still best-known as Ben Cropp the Shark Hunter, my passion for locating and diving on shipwrecks was far more lasting. From the moment I first dived, I dreamed of shipwrecks and treasure, and while I have probably found more wrecks in Australian waters than anyone else, I never did get my hands on much treasure.

These days if I found treasure I wouldn't be able to keep it anyway. It would become the property of the Australian government, but when I started diving on wrecks back in the early 1960s that wasn't the case. The rule then was "finders keepers" and it was a rule I made the most of.

In the years before bureaucracy stuck its nose in and spoilt all the fun, there were no restrictions on what we brought to the surface or how we got our hands on it.

I recovered so many interesting and historical artefacts that they filled my garage and, in 1981, I opened my Shipwreck Museum on the wharf at Port Douglas, where thousands of people gained an appreciation of our nautical history. The museum didn't make me any real money, just enough to keep the doors open, but it fulfilled an important role. Yet just as the bureaucrats stopped me recovering interesting artefacts, they forced me to close my museum. The hundreds of fascinating pieces in my collection now sit locked away in storage boxes.

Just as I do when recalling my shark-hunting days, I always ask people to judge my plundering of wrecks in terms of what was considered acceptable at the time. In the early 1960s there were no restrictions on salvage and the shipwrecks around Sydney Harbour were seen not just as interesting diving spots, but potential income. These easily accessible

Memento of a shipwreck … Lynn dives down to the anchor of the Ben Ledi, *a Scottish sailing ship wrecked in the Abrolhos Islands off the WA coast in 1879. Next page: For "Playboy" I shot model Gina Allen holding a cannonball beside the anchor of Matthew Flinders' ship* Porpoise, *which was lost at Wreck Reef in 1803.*

wrecks were relatively recent and of little historical importance. They didn't carry treasure like gold bullion, but they did have quantities of metal fittings such as copper, brass and lead, which were of interest to scrap-metal dealers.

Back then I was teaching at Balgowlah High School in Sydney, obsessed with diving and trying to establish myself as a filmmaker. Money was tight and I was always looking for ways to make ends meet. As a national champion spearfisherman, I naturally saw fishing as a way to make extra cash. Sydney's shoreline was a virtually untouched marine park inhabited by masses of large fish. It was so rare for fish like big black cod and groper to see divers that they would swim up to us. I was earning thirteen pounds ($26) a week teaching and, on that wage, I couldn't afford a car let alone the petrol to run it. Fishing provided a means to an end, allowing me to continue diving and earn money doing it. Fish-and-chip shops would buy fresh reef fish for 20 cents a kilo and pay twice that for ocean fish such as mackerel. On an average day, I would drop into a shop on my way home and collect $10 for my catch. A very good day would see me take home as much as I earned for a week's teaching.

From fishing it was a natural progression to plundering the 20 or so wrecks lying around Sydney Harbour. Some were a source of old coins, the rest were valuable for their scrap metal. All we had to do was break it up and get it to the surface. Just as no licence was needed to salvage a wreck, none was needed to buy or use explosives. I found myself an unlikely co-worker named Bill and went into the weekend salvage business. Bill was the wildest character I have ever met and, believe me, I've met some wild ones. He worked at a local rubbish tip, but somewhere along the way, he had worked in mines and picked up some experience with explosives.

Our technique was effective, but unsophisticated. We would buy gelignite and head out to a wreck in my tinnie. I'd dive down and place the charges, swim back to the boat and Bill would set them off. I'd bring up the pieces of metal and at the end of the day we would take a trailer load to the wreckers.

Hardly surprisingly with an offsider like Bill, things didn't always run smoothly. After all, this was the only man I ever saw bitten by a dead shark. Bill had come along for the ride when we were doing some filming for Shark Safari at Seal Rocks, in NSW. I killed a big grey nurse and we brought it up on the beach. A crowd gathered around and Bill thought

A Taiwanese fishing junk sinks off Escape Reef – I didn't discover why.

he'd show off a bit. He put his hand in the shark's mouth, but he slipped, bumped its head and its jaws locked on his hand. Unfortunately, we didn't get it on film.

Needless to say, Bill wasn't big on safety procedures. Once I climbed into the boat as he let off some charges. As I looked up, I saw that another boat had arrived and anchored right over the wreck site and a diver was jumping into the water just as the explosion went off. I've never seen anything like it. The diver hit the water feet first and then just shot back up into the boat. It was like watching a film played in reverse. He started his motor, headed off and we never saw him again. After that experience, I bought Bill a plunger so he could have more time for a look around before he set off the charges. Soon afterwards I found a wreck off Dee Why and set some charges to blow off its propeller. I climbed into the boat and looked over just as Bill was about to lower the plunger. I screamed at him to stop. Bill had balanced the plunger on the rest of the gelignite, with the wires lying in water on the bottom of the boat. If he had lowered the boom before I stopped him you wouldn't be reading this now.

I dissolved my partnership with Bill soon afterwards, but not before we had retrieved some valuable booty from the ocean floor. One of our most fruitful wrecks was the *Dunbar*, which sank in 1857 while entering Sydney Harbour after an 81-day voyage from England. The clipper foundered on a reef at the foot of South Head with the loss of all but one of its 122 passengers and crew.

Lost in the wreck of the *Dunbar* were thousands of coins, mainly copper penny tokens, but also gold sovereigns. Over the years these had fused together in a conglomerate of rock, and Bill and I had to use gelignite to separate them. It was well worth it. I could sell one gold sovereign for the equivalent of a week's wages.

Another find was memorable, but for a different reason. In February 1887, the iron barque *Scottish Prince* ran aground on the Southport bar off the Gold Coast. Diving on the wreck in 1964, I found two bottles of whisky, corks intact. Back on dry land another diver and I pulled out a couple of glasses and decided to sample my find. Given that it would have been at least 12 years old before it was placed on the ship, we were probably drinking the oldest and most potent whisky in the world. We uncorked one and it smelled awful, but we held our noses and took a sip. A quarter of a bottle later, we were both totally wiped out. We never did drink the rest of the bottle, and I haven't been able to face a whisky since.

Just as my whisky-drinking days ended in the mid-1960s, so did

The ghostly remains
of the Liberty ship
Francis Preston Blair
on Saumarez Reef.
Photo by Lynn Cropp.

my salvage operations. I have never lost my interest or love of finding shipwrecks and continue searching for sunken ships today, but I never again used gelignite to destroy a wreck in order to sell it for scrap. It wasn't because I didn't need the money or that the regulations had changed. It was just because I realised it was wrong. Besides, there were plenty of equally exciting adventures to be had looking for treasure – and they were a whole lot safer without Bill by my side.

Needles in a haystack

JUST ABOUT EVERYONE who ever straps on an air tank or a pair of flippers dreams of one day diving down and finding an old wreck crammed with treasure. The reality is not quite that simple. It can be difficult enough to find any wreck, let alone one that still holds treasure. Believe me, I've tried. I would estimate I have found more than 100 shipwrecks over the years and, more often than not, it required far more research than luck. One of the first things I learned about searching for buried treasure was this: X never marks the spot.

My usual technique was to find the name of a specific ship and then follow the paper trail until I had narrowed down the location to as small an area as possible. Typically I would read about a ship being wrecked in a historical feature in a newspaper report or old book. I would then head to State libraries, such as the Mitchell Library in Sydney or the John Oxley Library in Brisbane, and find every piece of information I could. Armed with all the clues, such as maps or eyewitness reports, I would head off to find my needle in a haystack.

In some areas this was easier than others. Searching for wrecks on the Great Barrier Reef was often just a matter of commonsense. Most ships had run aground and broken up on the outer reef as the crew tried to find an entrance through the reef. Knowing that, it was a case of using the best techniques to find the remains.

The simplest of these was to wear Polaroid sunglasses and look for black marks and lines in the coral, or shapes with sharp edges. The marks might have been where the anchor chain had run across the reef; sometimes we even found the anchor. The most telling signs were ballast stones. These were smooth stones stored in the ship's hold to be thrown overboard to lighten the ship, and their presence was a sure sign of a ship in trouble. Either they had been ditched by the crew or, if the ship sank, they were all that survived as it broke up around them.

Lynn photographed with another anchor, this one from the Ferguson, *which hit Ferguson Reef in 1840.*

An effective way to find such signs was to tow a diver behind the boat on a manta board. Similar in appearance to a child's boogie board, a manta board can skim along the surface of the water or dip below it. The diver would be on the lookout for a pile of ballast rocks or some other possible sign, and could dip down for a better look.

Another method I used was to ask trawler skippers to share their local knowledge with me. Professional fishermen mark every obstacle they hook up because snagged lines or torn nets cost them money. More often than not, the snag would be caused by a "wonky" hole, an underwater spring, but it also might just be the wrecked ship I was searching for.

The most tiresome method of pinpointing a wreck is to use a deep-water sounder. Similar to the old sonar navigation system, the sounder is painfully slow and often deceptive. I would circle the boat for hour after hour, driving my companions crazy with boredom, and when we finally picked up something on the sounder it could turn out to be nothing but fish.

And finally, when all else failed there was plain old dumb luck. In the 1970s I came across a newspaper article about a ship named *Aarhus*, which had sunk in Queensland waters in the 1880s. Through my researches, I became convinced that she had sunk after hitting a reef off Cape Moreton near Moreton Island and I set off to find her.

My shipmate on the voyage was my girlfriend of the time and, as I steered my boat slowly in the direction of Cape Moreton, she lay on the fly-bridge sunbaking. With the search area still a few kilometres away, I thought I might join her. I looked around to make sure there was no traffic, put the boat on automatic pilot and turned to leave the wheel. It was one of those amazing flukes you wouldn't believe if it hadn't happened to you. As I turned, I just happened to look over the side and spotted a black patch on the ocean floor. I immediately swung the boat around, anchored and there in 24 metres of water, two kilometres from where I intended to search, was the *Aarhus*, untouched for almost a century.

Who said you can't find a needle in a haystack?

Lynn and Ron Bell (above) looking for Kimberley diamonds. Right, Lynn examines the bottom section of the bilge pump at the wreck of the Fatima. *I found the wreck in 1977, but not its gold.*

Ships in the coral

Lynn with Dutch guilders from the wreck of the Batavia; *Bob Dickson with salvaged bottles from the* Cambus Wallace.

MY CHANCE DISCOVERY of the *Aarhus* brought me treasure of sorts – a $1,000 reward from the Federal Government and a large haul of artefacts such as one dozen brass alarm clocks in perfect condition. In those days, you were required to declare any discoveries to the Receiver of Wrecks, which was part of the Department of Home Affairs. You would tell them what you had recovered, they would write back and say they would be in touch and you never heard from them again. All of which led to my garage getting fuller and fuller and the eventual establishment of my Shipwreck Museum.

But much as the alarm clocks gained me some publicity and added to my collection, I was after something far more valuable. Bitten by the treasure-hunting bug, I was always hopeful that the jackpot lay just beyond the next reef. Or the next, or the next.

The waters off the east coast of Australia are the graveyard of many old ships, but few of these offer the hope of finding any real treasure. Most of those wrecked on the east coast originated from England and rarely carried anything of great value. The real treasure ships were Dutch galleons and they were more likely to have been wrecked on Australia's west coast. I had dived on a number of these west coast wrecks and found some Spanish coins and Dutch guilders, but nothing that would make me rich, so I kept searching elsewhere. My research told me there were still three undiscovered wrecks on the far north-east coast that could be carrying treasure, so I made these my target.

The first of these was the *Sun*, sunk in 1826 carrying Spanish silver dollars worth $30,000 to $40,000 at the time and many millions today. Contemporary reports had the *Sun* running aground on Boot Reef in the far north Coral Sea, but my calculations told me it was more likely to have been further south on Ashmore Reef. I found the wreck with reasonable ease just where I thought it would be, but, in three trips to the site, I found nothing apart from a few loose coins. On the last trip, Lynn Roberts, my partner for five years – we got together a few years after my third marriage ended – accompanied me as we filmed a TV special, *Search for Sunken Treasures*. Lynn was a graceful diver and we swam around two cannon, two anchors and a pile of ballast, but could only find a few silver dollars. My final thought as I gave up on the wreck was: "Who got here before me?"

In time I came to the conclusion that the *Sun* was the source of a fabulous 1880s discovery, which became known as Jardine's Treasure. Torres Strait Islanders fishing for bêche-de-mer spotted a dark shape underwater and, as they pulled up their anchor, it dislodged what they thought was a rock. In reality it was a massive conglomerate of coins. The man in charge of the fishing expedition was named Jardine, a police commissioner from a settlement at the tip of Cape York. Jardine said the treasure had been found at Boot Reef. I managed to get hold of a mud map he had made of the site. It matched the wreck I had found on Ashmore Reef perfectly, which just went to confirm one of the unwritten rules of treasure-hunting: never tell anyone the exact location of your find, in case you want to go back.

The second of the three ships was *Anne*, which had sunk, together with her sister ship *Druid*, on Cockburn Reef south of Cape York in 1853. The paper trail showed that *Anne* was carrying a cargo of "species", which referred to some sort of bullion, perhaps gold or silver ingots. Whatever it was, it sparked my imagination. I made several attempts to find the wreck, but it always evaded me. There are a total of nine shipwrecks on Cockburn Reef and I found two of them, but not *Anne*, the one I wanted. The closest I came was in 2002. I had towed diver Bob Dickson on a manta board for hours up and down that reef when he spotted a pile of ballast rocks. We dived again and again, pulling away rocks and heavy seaweed without luck, and finally I had to admit defeat.

Once again I had to ask, "Who got here first?" and once again I got my answer. The following year an old fisherman told me a story. Early last century some Torres Strait Islanders, who were diving for trochus shells near the reef north-east of Cape Grenville, came across a huge pile of gold. Under the direction of the local missionary, they took it to an island and buried it. At a later date, the missionary returned in his little sloop, recovered the gold and used it to further his work in New Guinea. Usually I don't take much notice of local myths but, given my research and the fact that the fisherman pinpointed a spot very close to where we found the ballast rocks, I am willing to believe this one could be true. Besides, it is a lot less painful than believing I had spent years trying to find a treasure that never existed.

Two down, one to go. The *Fatima* had sunk on Great Detached Reef, east of Cockburn, in 1854 with 18,000 ounces of gold on board. Again, the paperwork wasn't specific. The gold could have been in the form of ingots,

*Spoils of the deep
(clockwise from right):
Lynn with lanterns
salvaged from the
wreck of the 1903 ship
Yongala; Scruffy, first
of my three terriers,
beside the Yongala
bell; polishing brass
alarm clocks salvaged
from the 1880s
Aarhus wreck which
I discovered off Cape
Moreton, Qld.*

which would be quite visible, or dust, which would be lost forever.

The captain of the *Fatima* had survived and given the location of the wreck, and the Queensland Museum had searched for it unsuccessfully, so I had plenty of information to work on when I set out in 1977. Unfortunately, or so it seemed at the time, I had no more luck than the experts from the museum. I found seven wrecks on the reef, but none that matched the captain's log. It was 27 years later that it finally twigged that one of those seven wrecks was actually the *Fatima*, but in a different position from what I had expected. This time I was with my sons Dean and Adam and Trina Fleischmann, and we conducted the most thorough search possible, but could not come up with a speck of gold.

I had to wonder whether someone had found the treasure before us, as with the other two treasure ships. Perhaps our lack of success was for the best. Finders aren't keepers these days.

That ended my east coast search for buried treasure, but not my dreams of one day stumbling across a lost fortune. The ultimate find would be the wreck of the *Madagascar*, which left Melbourne bound for England in 1853 and was never heard of again. The ship was carrying 68,390 ounces of gold, plus wealthy passengers who had struck it rich on the goldfields and were taking their loot home. The cargo alone would be worth $35 million today, making it the seagoing treasure hunters' equivalent of Lasseter's Reef.

There is a story that an old woman on her deathbed claimed to have been a nurse on the *Madagascar*. She had survived after a mutiny off the coast of Brazil. Perhaps she was telling the truth and there is only one way we will ever know. That's why every time I come across an undiscovered wreck I ask the question, "Could this be the *Madagascar*?" And that's why, like every old pirate, I'll never stop hoping.

My sons Dean and Adam inspect an iron cannon from the Sun. *The wreck yielded a treasure of over 30,000 Spanish coins in the late 19th century.*

All that glitters is not gold

WHILE I HAVE YET TO FIND the fabulous treasure I have always dreamed of, many of my finds have been of incalculable value in historic terms. Even those without much historical value have provided me with memories and experiences beyond measure.

And failing that, there is always bound to be a good story or two.

My greatest disappointment as a wreck hunter was failing to discover six cannon jettisoned from Captain James Cook's the *Endeavour*. On June 10, 1770, during Cook's first voyage around the world, the *Endeavour* hit coral on the Great Barrier Reef and started to take in water. Cook ordered the ship's ballast and six cannons thrown overboard and, despite numerous attempts to recover them, they lay undiscovered for almost 200 years.

In 1969, just months before Cook's bicentennial celebrations, I used my life savings of $1,500 to finance an expedition to retrieve the cannon. Another team, from The Academy of Natural Sciences in the US, was headed for the area so there was no time to waste.

On the way I picked up a new magnetometer and a back-up diver. Both cost the same amount – nothing – and, in retrospect, both were overpriced. The German-made magnetometer, which I borrowed, was the latest word in detecting metal objects under the sea, but unfortunately, the instructions were in German and the fellow I found to translate them managed to do it back to front. As for my "assistant", the one thing I remember about him was that every second word he said was "bloody".

At one stage I interviewed him on film and, despite pleading with him not to use the b-word, he just couldn't do it and his language made the interview unusable. This was 1969, and if I had included the footage, I would have needed so many beeps that people would think I was interviewing Flipper.

After being stranded on a small island for a week as a storm blew itself out, we found some ballast in the search area without much trouble and started trailing the magnetometer, hoping it would pinpoint the cannon.

Lynn in the wreckage (right) of a Vultee Vengeance aircraft that ditched at Ruby Reef in 1944; and displaying the ancient coins she found on the wreck of the Batavia.

We cruised up and down the site for some time, my co-diver sitting at the back of the boat drinking beer while I steered and listened for the magnetometer to give a signal. Suddenly it produced a loud "ping" noise. I turned around excitedly, only to discover that my so-called helper had been leaving a trail of empty beer cans in our wake. In disgust, I suggested he might like to refrain from setting off the equipment, at which point he shrugged and went to sleep.

There were no further readings from the magnetometer so I turned to Plan B: diving down and swimming along the coral, looking for irregular shapes and rust stains. It was here in the murky water that I came face to face with a large whaler shark, which upset my concentration. Instead of being able to focus totally on the bottom of the reef, I kept looking out for the shark.

It was only a month or so later, long after I had been forced to call off my search, that I found out my magnetometer had indeed pinpointed Cook's cannon. My shipmate's beer can was aluminium and, as an alloy, could not have set off the machine.

The American team had no such problems. Obviously the instructions on their magnetometer were written in English. When they had searched the same spot without luck, the expert operating the machine told them, "No, that's the spot. Look again." They found the cannon overgrown by a metre of coral.

There is a postscript though. Years later I went back to the site to collect some ballast stones for my Shipwreck Museum and spotted a piece of metal the Americans had missed. It was what was called an "apron of lead", which was placed over the shot hole of the cannon to keep the powder dry, so I did end up with part of Cook's cannon.

As for what happened to my beer-drinking mate, I don't bloody know.

Another shipwreck that produced little treasure but plenty of memories was the *Batavia*. The story of the *Batavia* is one of the most bloodthirsty chapters in Australia's early history. A Dutch galleon, it sank on Morning Reef near Beacon Island west of Geraldton in Western Australia in 1629. Dozens of passengers and crew drowned trying to reach the island, but most managed to scramble ashore. Leaving merchant Jeronimus Cornelisz in charge of the survivors, the *Batavia*'s captain took the ship's boat and a small crew and sailed off to get help. Cornelisz, hoping to get his hands on the ship's bullion, led a mutiny in which 125 men, women and children

Dean checks out a Japanese gun on a WWII wreck in Micronesia.

were butchered. Others fought back, holding off the mutineers until help arrived.

Despite its grisly past, the *Batavia* is a popular diving spot known around the world. But in 1977 when I anchored nearby as part of my round-Australia expedition, it was largely untouched by amateur divers.

Already at the wreck when we arrived was a team of archaeologists from the Western Australian Museum. They were retrieving items from the wreck, and when we offered to help they readily accepted – on the proviso that anything we recovered went straight into the museum coffers.

My wife, Lynn, dived down and fanned the sand with her hands, exposing old coins one after the other. They were everywhere. We couldn't believe how easy it was. As soon as we grabbed them, one of the museum divers took them from us and put them into his "loot bag".

Well, that was the theory anyway. One of my divers came up and was immediately asked by one of the museum staff: "Have you got any coins?"

"No," he said. "I gave them to that bloke with the loot bag."

"Hmm," said the archaeologist. "Well, what are those round mounds under your wet suit?"

My diver shrugged, undid his suit and it sounded like a poker machine jackpot as the coins hit the deck. Even the museum people had to laugh.

That dive was incredibly exciting for us. We had finally dived on a real treasure ship and found treasure. One of the coins was dated 1598, which, given that Cook didn't discover the east coast until 1770, certainly gave us a new perspective on Australian history.

And the fact that we didn't get to keep any of our bounty? Well, as we were to find out, once the paper shufflers in the bureaucracy had finished with us it wouldn't have been worth our while anyway.

Sunken treasure (clockwise from top): Lynn and Wally inspect the Pandora *cask; Eva, Gina Allen and Bob Dickson uncover cannonballs on Wreck Reef; me with a Spanish "piece of eight" at Ashmore Reef.*

Opening Pandora's box

THE MOST significant discovery of my career was the wreck of the HMS *Pandora*. As well as being the oldest known shipwreck on Australia's east coast, it had a close link with one of the most famous of all nautical tales, the mutiny on the *Bounty*.

The *Pandora*, a 24-gun frigate, was the ship sent from England under the command of a Captain Edwards to capture the 14 *Bounty* mutineers still in Tahiti. The first part of the mission went to plan, with the mutineers rounded up and locked in a cage on the ship's deck. Not surprisingly, the cage became known as Pandora's Box.

But on August 28, 1791, the *Pandora* was swept onto a detached coral outcrop as it tried to cross the Great Barrier Reef into Torres Strait. Over the next four hours, the crew dropped ballast and pumped frantically, but at dawn it was obvious the ship was going down. The crew crammed into four boats or grabbed anything that would float. Despite the captain's orders to let the prisoners drown, the Master at Arms threw them the keys to their chains as he abandoned ship. Four of the mutineers and 31 crew drowned.

The survivors gathered on a small sand cay, which they called Wreck Island, and three days later set off in the four small boats, eventually reaching Timor.

When I arrived at the site 186 years later in my first big boat, *Beva*, a 48-foot Grand Banks, I could see immediately what Edwards and his crew had faced: strong currents, tide rips, rough seas and deep water. We stopped counting the sharks when we reached 100 on the first day. It was immediately obvious that a detailed underwater search for the wreck was impossible.

With the assistance of then Minister for Defence Jim Killen, I was able to enlist the help of the Royal Australian Air Force to make a four-hour aerial search with a magnetometer in three weeks' time.

 *Wally Gibbons ties up a clay cask from the* Pandora. *Photo by Lynn Cropp.*

Another expedition, led by American Steve Domm on the *Reverie*, was due in the area at the time of the aerial search, and I was desperate to find the wreck before they got there. We spent the intervening three weeks combing the area, and found over 20 other wrecks but not the *Pandora*. Finally, we had to drop anchor and wait for the *Reverie* and the RAAF to show up.

Steve Domm's team arrived the day before the aerial search was scheduled and I brought him up to date with the arrangements I had made with the RAAF.

For three and a half hours, the RAAF Neptune swept over the site without picking up any signal on the magnetometer. As a last resort, I radioed the pilot to try searching a coral outcrop at the extreme southern edge of the search area. It was the very first site I had dived on three weeks earlier without luck, but I figured it was worth a try.

The pilot's voice crackled over my radio: "Got a good one!" The plane dropped smoke flares over the spot and we sailed full-speed-ahead to drop our own heavily anchored marker buoys. Divers from both *Beva* and *Reverie* quickly put on their gear and jumped into the water as the Neptune pilot dipped his wings and headed back to base in Townsville.

The first diver from my team to go down was my nephew, Ron Bell. As he surfaced, I looked at him hopefully. He shook his head. Nothing but sand and sharks. I asked how many sharks he had seen.

"Only about 30," he called back as I prepared to take my turn.

Like Ron and our co-diver, Wally Gibbons, I saw nothing but sharks and sand. Anxiously looking over at the *Reverie*, I could tell they were having no luck either. As the sun went down, we all called it a day.

Before we left the site for calmer waters, I remember looking around, wondering where the wreck could be. The RAAF reading meant it was definitely close by, but where? I spotted a coral bommie not far ahead. Suddenly it was all clear: We were looking on the wrong side of the reef. The *Pandora* must have hit this outcrop of coral and continued another 200 metres or so before it sank. I made a mental note of the spot and told Ron: "I'll put you right on the wreck tomorrow."

Early the next morning I dropped anchor over the spot and had Ron follow the anchor chain down. There was no time to lose. *Reverie* was doing a sweep using its magnetometer and would pass over our anchor in another five or 10 minutes. I knew that once we found the wreck both teams would be credited with the discovery, but for reasons of personal pride I still wanted to be first.

Dianne Costa and Lin Sutherland swim over the wreck of a Japanese Mitsubishi Zero aircraft in the Louisiade Archipelago.

My previous boat Call
of the Wild *anchored
off the wreck of the*
Corea *at Eel Reef.*

In a couple of minutes Ron surfaced in a cloud of bubbles and
excitedly confirmed that the *Pandora* was lying next to our anchor. I
jumped on the radio and broke the news to Steve. Together, both teams
dived down to inspect our discovery and film the amazing sight.

It was like a time capsule: an almost intact British man-o'-war lying in
30 metres of water, waiting for more than 180 years to tell us about our
past. A giant anchor lay next to the anchor of the *Beva*. Cannons were
everywhere, some as long as two metres and weighing almost 200 kilos.
We spotted a huge iron box, and there was great excitement. As always,

thoughts of treasure sprang to mind and, as always, they were dashed. The giant box turned out to be an iron stove! We disturbed little on the wreck, being well aware of its historical significance, but did bring up a few artefacts, including a large stoneware cask, as proof of our find.

Two days later, the Ministry for Home Affairs declared the *Pandora* a historic shipwreck to protect it from looters. Without so much as a thank you, the ministry cabled me on my boat, telling me to get off the wreck. It would be six years before another diver, financed this time by the Queensland government and employed by the Queensland Museum, would set eyes on the *Pandora*, but my involvement with the wreck was ongoing and only confirmed my deep mistrust of bureaucrats.

Two years after we had found the most significant wreck on Australia's east coast, the government finally saw fit to present Steve and I with our reward – the princely sum of $5,000 each, which covered about half our out-of-pocket expenses.

To add insult to injury, the Federal Taxation Department then stepped in and demanded I pay half that in tax, making me the first person in the country's history to be taxed on a government reward. I fought that ruling for three years and, while it proved costly, I had the satisfaction of winning my case and receiving an apology from the Treasurer.

The *Pandora* tax issue was but a small part of my problems with pen pushers and paper shufflers. The small number of relics I had brought back from HMS *Pandora* were to be key exhibits at the Shipwreck Museum I planned to open at Port Douglas. In the meantime, I lent them to a government-funded museum in Brisbane. When I was ready to open my museum, I called the museum to arrange transport. My jaw nearly hit the floor when I was informed that the Minister for Home Affairs was refusing to return the pieces.

There followed another long and costly fight, and this one I did not win. It rankles that the items I found at my own expense and retrieved two days before the government even knew of the wreck's existence sat on public view without any acknowledgement of my part in their discovery. That's bureaucracy for you. Their petty rules and interference made things difficult for me, but nothing could ever dampen my enthusiasm for the sea and for the life it has given me.

 *I found this lamp on the wrecked* Scottish Prince. *Photo by Lynn Cropp.*

Pay for play

AS THE SUCCESS of my films increased, I was in the wonderful position of being paid to play at my hobbies. I loved to explore and to search for shipwrecks. If I wanted to go to a certain location in the hope of finding a wreck that I had researched or if I wanted to see some marine life I had read about I would go to my usual clients and sell them the idea of making a film about the expedition. Usually they would agree and the film budget would finance the trip. That was the beauty of what I was doing. There was nothing scripted about my films. I had an idea of where I was going, but it was the getting there, not just the destination, which made the film interesting. If something unexpected happened – and it always did – that was in the film. If something funny or dangerous or unusual occurred – and again, it always did – that was in there, too. I think that is one of the reasons people liked the films so much: because they could see that they were real and they were able to put themselves in my shoes and really experience what my family and I were experiencing.

When Ron Taylor and I started making films, our intention was to show Australians the amazing underwater world at their doorstep, but in the years that followed I was also able to show that world to viewers in the United States, Europe and Japan. I did all my own selling direct to the distributors and, in that way, I was able to build personal relationships which lasted more than 30 years.

My main market in Australia was the Seven Network, providing films for their series The World Around Us. My friends at Seven were always first port of call and, once I had them tied up, I would head overseas. In Tokyo a friend introduced me to Mr Ushiyama, a producer who had not one but three wildlife shows on Japanese television. He bought documentaries from filmmakers all over the world and I supplied all his marine films, which were then re-cut and screened with a Japanese commentary. It was the same in Germany where I sold to the Kirsch

 *As I tickle a potato cod at the Cod hole, Lynn takes our picture.*

network, which then distributed my films throughout Europe. In the US I offered my films to all the networks, but my biggest client was Disney, which liked my family adventures but wouldn't buy my "nasties" about tiger sharks or box jellyfish. The last thing Disney wanted was to give small children nightmares.

I sold my films on the basis of a 50 per cent fee up-front, which meant I never had to put my own money into a production, and I never took a single hand-out from the government in more than 40 years and more than 100 films. Such an arrangement also allowed me to remain independent. Only once was I tempted to "go corporate". In the early 1980s, Ivan Tors, creator of the enormously successful TV series *Sea Hunt* and *Flipper*, was in his sixties and wanting to wind down his hands-on involvement in his company. He asked me to come in as his partner and teach his two sons the business so they could take over when he retired. He made me a very attractive offer, which would have set me up financially for life. After much consideration, I decided no amount of money could compensate for the loss of freedom to make my own films when and how I wanted. It proved to be one of the best decisions of my life. Ivan Tors died soon afterwards and I would have been left as the partner of two young men with no experience but plenty of say in how things would be run.

Throughout the '70s, '80s and '90s, I made at least two films a year. In 1977 I signed a contract with Seven to make a series called The Rugged Coast which required five shows a year for two years. It was my busiest period, but it also provided me with the greatest experiences of my professional life.

My golden run as a documentary-maker lasted until 2002 when I was hit with a series of setbacks. First was the collapse of the Kirsch group, my European distributors. Kirsch went down with debts of about $7 billion, so the exposure of Ben Cropp Productions didn't cause a ripple at their end, but I felt as if my office in Queensland had been hit by a tidal wave. I had signed a $1.4 million contract with Kirsch and had restructured my business accordingly, investing a great deal to upgrade my production facilities. Luckily I had received $400,000 up-front, but it

A whaler shark, one of a large group found all around Australia, caught up in a shark net. Next page: For one of my films, the Cropp family spent a week marooned on Forbes Island, living on mudcrabs, coconuts and fish caught with a primitive pole spear. Photo by Lynn Cropp.

still left a huge hole. At the same time, the Seven Network simply stopped buying documentaries because of over-supply. The reality TV boom had seen the market for docos drop by two-thirds and, as if that weren't bad enough, my market was suddenly flooded with a whole new generation of documentary-makers armed with inexpensive digital cameras. Where once a filmmaker needed to make a substantial investment in film and equipment before setting out, now all that was needed to be in business was a $7,000 camera off the shelf.

All this combined to force me into semi-retirement for two years and it is only now that I have bounced back with a run of new contracts for Australian television networks. I accept that the golden age of documentary-making in this country has passed and, while I am sad to see it go, I count myself incredibly lucky to have come along when I did. To be able to roam the world for 40 years and make a good living doing so has been a blessing.

I have seen and experienced things that others can only dream about, at the time and place of my choosing, and alongside the people I liked and admired most.

Right, as part of a "Playboy" shoot, I photographed model Gina Allen feeding fish at Heron Island. Left, Gayle Flieschmann lost her bikini top to a dolphin.

Marine mosaic

IT MAY SEEM like an unlikely partnership – the seafaring adventurer with an eye for the ladies and the flamboyant gay entertainer best known for colourful shirts and camp stage performances – but it worked.

Peter Allen was one of the best-known entertainers in the world in the mid-1970s and '80s. His hit songs such as *I Go To Rio* and *Tenterfield Saddler*, his shows at Radio City Music Hall in New York and his Oscar-winning songwriting had made him a household name. As his signature song *I Still Call Australia Home* so beautifully illustrates, most of his time was spent in the US, but his heart always belonged to Australia.

His main home was in Los Angeles, but whenever he needed a break he would head to his house at Oak Beach, near Port Douglas. He owned a lovely beach house with magnificent views of the ocean and he was a real disciple of the North Queensland lifestyle. It was as a fellow resident of Port Douglas that I first met Peter and, as I got to know him better, I had a brainwave. I was always looking for ways to market my documentaries, and Peter was the ultimate showman, and always looking for ways to reach a broader audience. I had the idea of joining forces, with Peter becoming "host" of my films. I put it to Peter and his manager, and they jumped at the idea, Peter because he thought it sounded like fun, and his manager because it would be a change from Peter's on-stage persona.

Basically, once I had planned or perhaps even finished most of filming for a documentary, I would contact Peter and work in with his schedule. He and his partner, Greg, would come out on the boat with us for up to a week and I would film an opening and closing with Peter. The film would then be marketed along the lines of "Peter Allen Presents …"

There was very little money in the partnership for Peter, but he didn't care. He just loved coming out on the boat and enjoying experiences that were a world away from his Hollywood lifestyle. He was the sort of person who could see the humour in just about any situation and being out in the wild in Australia provided some great material for him. Our most successful film together was titled *The Deadliest Creature on Earth*

 *Never too young to fish: Laughlan Island children with the day's catch.*

and was about the box jellyfish. For the opening sequence, I had Peter
stand in some mangroves and recite from the script as I filmed. The script
went something like this: "These are mangroves, the natural habitat of the
deadliest creature on earth…" The next line was supposed to be "… the
box jellyfish" But instead, Peter looked up and said, "… so what the f--k
am I doing here!" We all laughed so much that he incorporated the line
into his stage act.

Peter and Greg were always great fun to have on the boat, and my kids
really loved them.

I think one of the reasons Peter enjoyed doing the films so much
was that it gave him a chance to get away from the plastic world of show
business. I have always believed that the best way to get to know someone
is on a boat. No telephones, no posturing, no bull. Everyone is equal and
the real person comes through. Two other Hollywood celebrities who
sailed on my boat were Clint Eastwood and Leonard Nimoy. Clint came
out for a day along with the chairman, president and vice-president of
Warner Bros. At the time I was trying to do a deal for a feature film, along
with a North Queensland neighbour, Diane Cilento, and her husband,
Tony Shaffer. Tony was a top playwright – his best-known play is *Sleuth* –
and writer, and he was going to write the script. We had a great day on the
boat with Clint and the Warner Bros bosses. They loved the idea for the
film, and it was handshakes and back-pats all round. When they headed
off, I said to Diane, "I think we've got it." But nothing ever came of it.
That's feature films for you.

Leonard Nimoy was another of my "hosts" and featured on 12 of
my films. Unlike the deal with Peter Allen, which I put together myself,
Leonard was signed up by my US distributor, but just as had happened
with Peter, once we met and he came out on the boat we got along well.
Over the years, I had the boss of IBM – then the world's biggest company
– and his wife on the boat. Another time we were moored alongside
Rupert Murdoch's boat and went aboard for a drink. Imagine trying to get
a meeting with people like that on dry land. It would be impossible, but
among boaties, it just happens.

Peter Allen and I did many great films together over the years.
When *The Deadliest Creature on Earth* screened, it was the highest-
rating documentary in Australian television history. But even more than

Eva dives with a massive manta ray at Lady Musgrave Island.

*The manta ray
appears oblivious to its
bikini-clad swimming
companion.*

the ratings, I enjoyed working with Peter because he was always so enthusiastic and full of fun.

Two other fun guests were Barry Humphries and Lady "Kanga" Tryon, one-time girlfriend of Prince Charles. Lady Tryon was an aristocrat with an Aussie background, thus her nickname, Kanga. She might have had a title in front of her name, but she swore like a trooper so we got on well.

I took Barry and Kanga to a special shark hole, a place where at low tide half a dozen whaler sharks would circle in a small coral pool, waiting for the tide to rise so they could swim out and prowl the coral. Finding sharks in a situation like this and being able to swim safely above them is an unforgettable experience, and Barry was ecstatic. Lady Tryon wasn't quite so enthusiastic and refused to get into the water. I did what any self-respecting colonial would do, and pushed her in. She came out after her swim bubbling with excitement and very happy, saying she would make mention of it in her biography – suitably embellished of course. It was only later that I thought about the consequences of what I had done, but it all turned out well. Lady Tryon even told me she had only two loves in her life: Prince Charles and me. I'm still not sure if that was a compliment.

Peter Allen, Clint Eastwood, Lady Kanga, Dame Edna … who would have thought it when I was growing up in Tweed Heads?

Marine mosaic:
a brightly marked
cleaner shrimp blends
into its highly coloured
surroundings.

This is your wives

IN 1979, TO MY SURPRISE, I was the subject of an episode of *This is Your Life*. I thought I was going along to Channel Seven to take part in a talk show, but all the while my wife, Lynn, had been working with the producers to come up with a guest list for a *This Is Your Life* on Ben Cropp.

The first people Lynn contacted were my two former wives, Van and Eva. Both jumped at the chance to surprise me, leading to the situation where I was on TV hugging and laughing with my three wives. Afterwards, to keep the party going, we all went out to dinner, where someone suggested the show should have been titled *This Is Your Wives*. When it was replayed several years later that was the title.

Remaining on good terms with one's ex-partners might seem strange, but I can honestly say I am still close friends with all three of my former wives. Lynn and I contact each other nearly every week. I'm in touch with Eva less regularly because she lives in the US, and with Van on significant dates such as birthdays and Christmas. It's just the wedding anniversaries that we tend to let slide.

Recently I took Van out to dinner and, even at the age of 60, she looked stunning, but then she always was a beautiful woman. We met in the Sydney beachside suburb of Collaroy in 1963. Van Laman was hard to miss – 18 years old, pretty, athletic and a great diver. We married a year later. I was nine years older than Van, but even so, I was too young for the commitment of marriage. Maybe I still am.

The thing that brought us together was our mutual love of the sea and diving. Van was an exceptional skindiver. I taught her how to spearfish and just six months later she won the Australian women's championship, beating Ron Taylor's wife, Valerie. I don't think Val ever got over it.

Van also made the *Guinness Book of Records* in the category "Largest Shark Killed by a Woman". Shark-hunting was big news in those days

 *Lynn kisses a dolphin at Monkey Mia, Western Australia, in 1978.*

and I promoted Van as "the mermaid who swims with sharks". The media lapped it up.

The only problem we had was with her mother. I've seen some ferocious man-eaters underwater, but Van's mum was up there with the best of them. She was certain that, like all men, I was out for all I could get from Van, and she convinced her daughter that she'd better get in, as in out, first. One day I got home from a marketing trip to the US to find that Van had left and cleaned me out. I mean really cleaned me out. I couldn't even find a bottle opener and I know for a fact we had two of them.

Van had skipped to New Zealand with a surfie known as "Bogangar Bob" in reference to his home break of Bogangar Head near Pottsville in northern NSW. Pretty soon Van realised that the only thing Bob owned – and then only briefly – was the wave he was riding. After a year she wanted to come back, but by then I had met another mermaid whose name was Eva Papp.

As a child in 1948, Eva had climbed beneath a barbed-wire border fence to escape communist Hungary and had settled with her parents on the Gold Coast. When I met her, she was 20 years old and had just been crowned Miss Gold Coast Charity Queen. The fact that she was also an accomplished scuba diver helped me make up my mind. I had always dreamed of sailing the seas in my own boat, as Hans Hass did with his beautiful wife, Lotte. In Eva, I felt I had found my Lotte.

Clockwise from above: with my first wife, Van, at our 1965 wedding; my second wife, Eva, inspects a whisky bottle recovered from the wreck of the Scottish Prince *off Southport; Laughlan Islanders dance in my honour on my return after 20 years to make* Islands Lost in Time.

Eva plays with a dolphin in the Porpoise Pool at Tweed Heads, NSW. Right, the fantastic emperor angel fish.

Eva and I had a happy eight years together, on one level as man and wife, on another as two adventurers discovering the world and making films of what we saw. Jacques Cousteau's boat *Calypso* became a major part of his films, as did *Beva*, the 48-footer named after me and Eva.

As a result of the many films we made in exotic locations, Eva in her skimpy bikini became one of the best-known women in Australia. So popular did she become that she was approached to do a pictorial spread for Playboy. When we met, Eva was the innocent, naive one, but she knew that if I heard about the Playboy shoot I would put a stop to it. So she didn't tell me until it was too late, simply handing me the magazine and saying, "Here Ben, have a look at this." I was shocked, but I couldn't be angry because she looked so good. I suppose I was amused by her daring, but looking back now I see it as a symptom of something deeper; after years of being part of a high-profile partnership, she wanted to make her mark as an individual.

Long after we split, Eva told me the thing she missed most about our days together was seeing the sun rise in the wild with me. We shared many unforgettable experiences and saw places together most couples could never even dream of, but after eight years she decided she needed to see the world through her own eyes. It was a sad parting, announced months in advance so we could share one last trip together. It was on the remote Gulf of Carpentaria that Eva and I saw our last sunrise together.

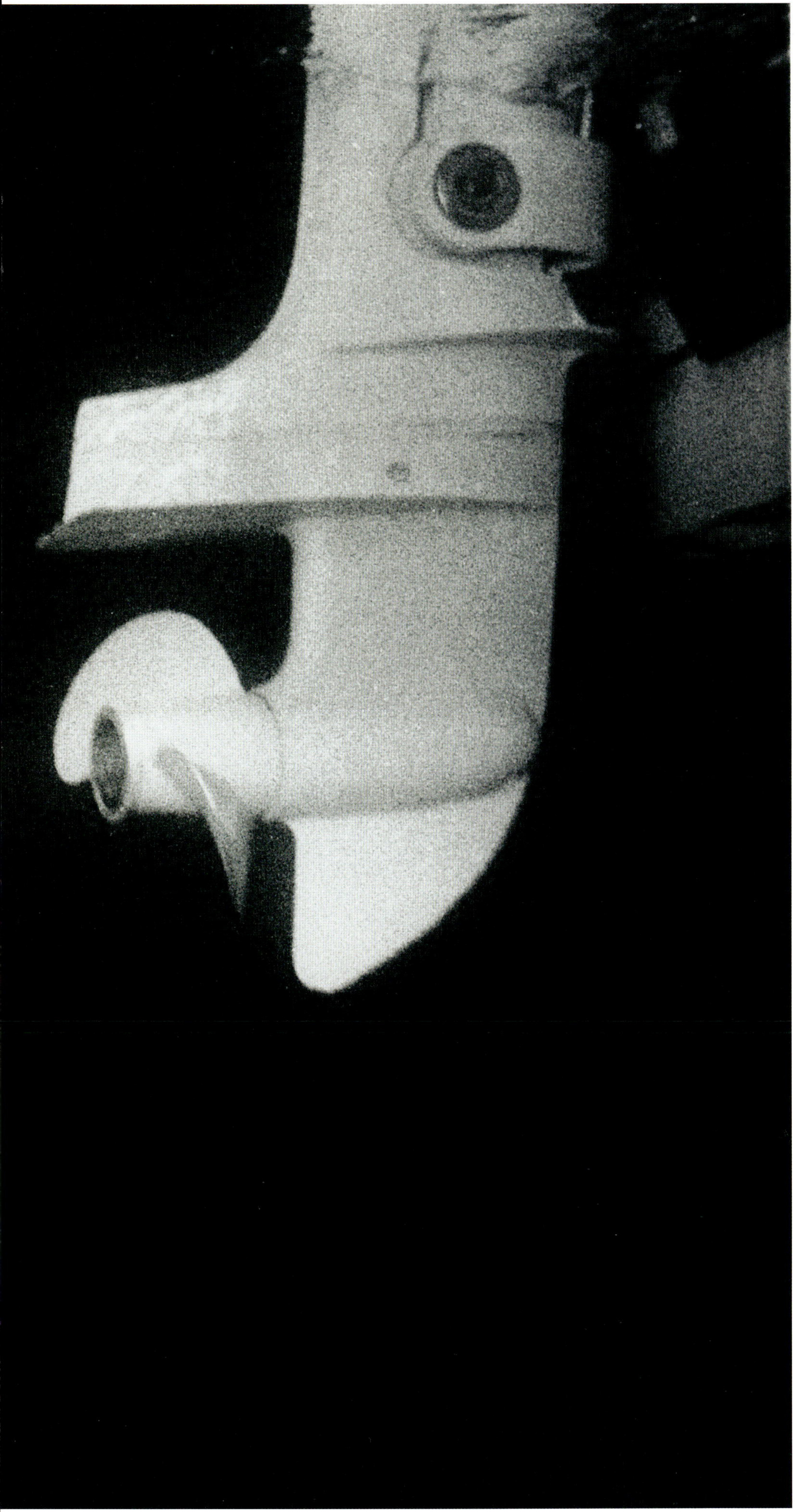

The way things were:
Tony Smith with
a 2.5m grey nurse
shark, which was
killed in 1963 with
a 12-gauge shotgun on
a hand spear.

Eva is now a born-again Christian and a wealthy woman. As she was growing up on the Gold Coast, her father was quietly buying up cheap farmland inland from Coolangatta. Needless to say, it is no longer farmland and no longer cheap. The proceeds from her father's astute real estate speculation have kept Eva and her church well.

Not long ago, she called me her "best mate", but she certainly knocked me for a loop when she left me. For six months, I drifted like a rudderless ship. I threw myself into the life of an eligible bachelor, but soon tired of it. I was lonely without Eva and longed for the love and companionship we had shared.

It was around this time that I met Lynn Patterson, who would become my third wife. Lynn was a Canadian nurse working in Australia. We were to have some wonderful times together, but the first couple of times we met were disastrous.

At the peak of my depression over losing Eva, I arranged to take a friend on a day trip on my boat. Knowing I was lonely, he suggested he bring along a young woman he thought I might hit it off with. Meanwhile, Eva contacted me to say she was coming back. I was thrilled, but the night before I was to take these people out on the boat she rang to say she had changed her mind. To say I wasn't the best company when we headed off next morning is an understatement. I was in a filthy mood and barely acknowledged Lynn all day. A week later I arranged to take the same friend out to Moreton Island on a four-day trip and, though I couldn't even remember her name, I suggested he bring Lynn along.

If the first trip was bad, this one was worse. My friend brought two women with him, knowing both were in love with him. When he started paying more attention to one, the other ran below deck and took an overdose of sleeping tablets. When I realised what had happened, I ran downstairs and pushed my fingers down her throat, causing her to bring up the pills – all over me – and saving her life. While I was doing this, the man of her dreams stood there stupidly, doing nothing to help.

When we got to Moreton Island, my friend, who was starting to annoy

Rhonda Smith dives with a tame dugong at Tanna Island in the New Hebrides.

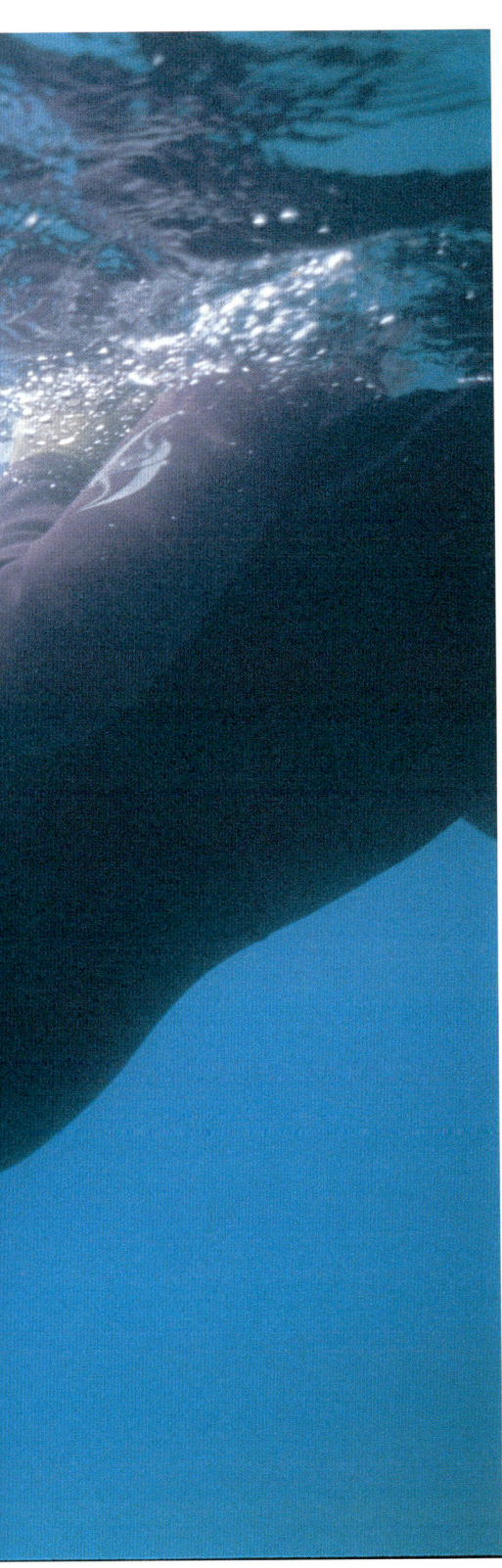

me more and more, thought it would be funny to write the word HELP in giant letters on the sandy cliff face. I was shocked when I saw what he had done and started looking to the sky in the hope that no passing plane had seen his message. Over the past few weeks, some idiot had been sending out hoax distress signals, and the police were on the look-out for him. "Quick," I told my now ex-friend. "Get rid of that right now." He just stood there laughing. By now I was furious. I went ashore and kicked sand all over the letters.

"Right, that's it," I said to him, back on the boat. "With a friend like you I don't need an enemy. Trip's over, we're going back." When we reached Paradise Waters, I ordered them all off the boat, saying I didn't want to see any of them again.

As for Lynn, I wasn't really interested in seeing her again either, even though she hadn't put a foot wrong during the trip. Just knowing that oaf had brought her along was enough for me to lump her in with him.

Luckily, another friend on the trip pulled me aside and told me that Lynn had really been impressed with the way I'd handled the girl overdosing and that she was as disgusted as I with my idiot guest. "She's a good kid," he said. "She's stayed back to help clean the boat. Why don't you ask her to stay for dinner?"

Well, I did ask her to stay for dinner and she stayed the next 18 years – the happiest and most contented years of my life.

A tame (and vegetarian) dugong clasps diver Jan Bochemski. In Australian waters, these animals are protected. Next page: A dugong surfaces to breathe. They can grow to 3m long, and their mouths are angled down to allow them to graze the seabed. Photos by Rhonda Smith.

Trip of a lifetime

SOMETIMES I feel as if I've lived those old Lucky Starr lyrics "'Cos I've been everywhere, man, I've been everywhere …" People often ask me the best trip I have ever been on, the best places I have seen and the most memorable experiences I have had, and they are nearly always surprised by the answer. I suppose they expect me to speak about some exotic overseas location in Europe or South America, but there is no question: The best voyage I ever took was the two years I spent circumnavigating Australia, following in the wake of Matthew Flinders.

I have always admired Flinders as Australia's greatest-ever navigator. In 1965 I was on an expedition, which discovered the remains of *Porpoise* and *Cato*, the boats he lost on Wreck Reef in 1803. It had been my dream to follow the route he took from 1801 to 1803, when he became the first person to circumnavigate Australia. In 1977 when Channel Seven agreed

Victim of headhunters with Spanish "pieces of eight" coins. Above, Adam jumps from a crashed DC3 plane in the Kimberley region.

to my proposal, the dream became reality. Seven would buy 10 one-hour programmes about the trip, to be packaged as a series called *This Rugged Coast*. It was the most ambitious project of my career and turned out to be far more of an experience than even I could have imagined.

When Lynn and I began our relationship, the start date for what would be a 15,000 nautical mile, two-year voyage of discovery had been scheduled for some time and was fast approaching. It seemed the most natural thing in the world that she should come along. Not too many women can boast they went on a two-year honeymoon. Even fewer can say that two other people came along for the ride. The other two members of the crew were famous old-time diver Wally Gibbons and my nephew Ron Bell, who would die tragically years later in a tractor accident. Choosing the team for a trip like this was obviously a very important job. Spending years together in close quarters can test the closest of friendships, but since my earliest days as a filmmaker, I had developed a successful system, which still works for me. The two most obvious attributes I look for in my companions are that they be good divers and camera operators. They also have to be what I call "action" people, meaning they must be adventurous and capable enough to have a go at just about anything which presents itself. And as we spent most of our time in swimming gear, it was also important to have a few attractive bodies on show – a prerequisite that Lynn filled admirably. A sense of fun is also imperative. It is all about getting the right mix both on and off camera, and on this trip it all came together perfectly.

It is almost impossible to sum up this incredible trip in a few pages. I even wrote a book about it, called *This Rugged Coast: Adventures Around Australia's Coastline*, published in 1980 and now long out of print.

We left the Gold Coast and sailed off anti-clockwise. The first highlight was finding the wreck of the HMS *Pandora*. Finding what is possibly Australia's most historic shipwreck was a fitting way to start our circumnavigation, but our adventures weren't isolated to what we found underwater. Many were on dry land. One of the most spectacular was at Groote Eylandt in the Gulf of Carpentaria, home of the Umbakumba people. I had heard of the Aboriginal form of justice known as "trial by spear" and always wanted to film it. With the help of the local policeman at Groote Eylandt, the Umbakumba people agreed to perform the ceremony, allowing it to be filmed for the first time. Trial by spear was used

An Australian wonderland ... Freedom III cruises
up the spectacular King George River gorge, in WA.

as punishment for men found guilty of such acts of betrayal as adultery or theft. The guilty man had to stand before the rest of the group as they threw spears at him. His only protection was a spear, which he used to ward off the flying missiles. The ordeal continued until blood was drawn, whether from a small nick or a fatal wound. It all depended on the agility of the target, the theory being that he would get what he deserved.

White authorities had banned this form of retribution several years earlier, but the Umbakumba men were well versed in the ceremony and more than happy to demonstrate their spear-throwing skills and to revive part of their traditional culture. It was a huge event for the locals, with the school closed so the children could watch. Obviously we didn't want anyone injured so padding was placed over the points of the spears, but a direct hit would still hurt.

The first man who took a turn at playing the target was remarkably deft. He would dodge from one side to the other and batter incoming spears away like a tennis champion at the net. The crowd, which numbered several hundred, loved it, laughing and cheering as if they were at a football match. The Umbakumba men threw themselves into the performance, providing great footage for me. Everyone involved was a volunteer, and it was obvious they enjoyed the opportunity. The Umbakumba were known as pretty tough men and, as much as showing off a traditional ceremony, they also jumped at the chance of displaying their courage, skill and manliness.

A place that made a huge impression was King George River Falls in the Kimberleys. I have no hesitation in calling it the most scenic spot in Australia and the only place in the Kimberleys where the water was clear enough to dive. A few years later, the millionaire adventurer Dick Smith was planning a helicopter flight around Australia and I told him he should go there. He did, and raved about it. At that time Dick Smith and I were two of only a small group of non-Aboriginal people to have seen the falls. Now they are a "must see" on every tourist operator's itinerary.

The area was famous for diamonds. We searched high and low and found plenty of crystals, but no diamonds. I did discover another treasure

The Umbakumba people of Groote Eylandt perform a ritual dance before re-enacting their traditional "Trial by Spear" for my camera.

though. As we took *Beva* up King George River, we came across a tiny pond which, when the tide went out, became the ultimate "barra hole". I have never seen so many barramundi in my life. It was a fisherman's dream. Unfortunately I made the mistake of telling a yachtie about it and he couldn't keep·his mouth shut either. After he had been there, he got on his radio and gave the location. By the time I managed to get back, it had been fished out. I'll never make that mistake again.

It was in the Kimberleys that we found the most magnificent Aboriginal rock art, especially Wandjina, or spirit, paintings. One, drawn along the roof of a cave, was a figure perhaps seven metres long. At Bigge Island we found an amazing cave painting depicting white men smoking pipes and wearing what looked like Dutch clothing, even down to wooden clogs. They were carrying pigskin bags to collect water and, in the background, was what looked like a Galliot, an oared vessel used in shallow waters. This was interesting on two counts. First, Aboriginal paintings usually portray tribal life, animals or spiritual matters. Second, the only Dutch explorer I knew of who had visited Bigge Island was Abel Tasman in 1644.

While in the Gulf of Carpentaria, we stumbled upon a burial cave where skulls and skeletons were placed in hollow logs. I took a photograph of Lynn holding a skull above one of the logs and wrote an article, which was published along with the photograph. By the time we reached Darwin, we were met with newspaper headlines that summed up our error in the politically incorrect language of the day: "Abos After Cropp". That, combined with another incident in which I was in more strife for disturbing some headhunters' trophies on Torres Strait Island, taught me a good lesson: never touch a burial site. It can lead to grave trouble.

Further south, we pulled into Montebello Islands, the site of the first British atomic tests in 1952 and 1956. I learned that, soon after World War II, some pearl luggers had anchored in the islands to collect pearl shells for "seeding" to grow cultured pearls. I was told they had found some very large shells, known as "clunkers". These were too big for cultured pearls, and they had thrown them back. Wally and I dived at the spot and found some of these giant shells, which measured more than 30 centimetres across. Knowing the shells had been thrown back in the 1940s, we were pretty excited as we opened them. Shell after shell produced nothing, but then we opened another, and it contained nine pearls, eight small and one large. Lynn had it set into a ring as a memento of our visit to Montebello Islands. In retrospect, we were lucky that was the only permanent reminder we took away with us. Incredible as it seems now, when the

Above, admiring rock art we found at Bigge Island, WA, which appears to show Dutch sailors in clogs, with pigskin waterbags and pipes. Right, at Bathurst Bay, we found this image of a pearl lugger (an 1899 cyclone wiped out the local pearling fleet). Photos by Lynn Cropp.

I found this pile of trophy heads on Simbo Island in the Solomon Islands, relics from the days of head-hunting. Photo by Lynn Cropp.

British announced plans for their atomic tests, Australians were delighted and even proud that Britain had chosen our country to test atomic bombs. Some 25 years later, attitudes had changed and I decided to shoot a segment of my film at Ground Zero, site of the explosions. For dramatic effect, we took along a Geiger counter. We had been assured the area was totally safe and clear of any radioactivity, but I thought it might make a good shot if the Geiger counter gave just a little reading. As soon as we switched it on, the needle on the dial went off the scale. We took the shot and raced straight back to the water's edge to scrub ourselves thoroughly. We were there only for a minute, but we wouldn't have been human if we didn't find ourselves worrying we had been contaminated. The only living creatures we saw at the site were a few cockroaches and ants – and the ants all lived underground. They'd learnt their lesson.

From then on, any unexplained ailment one of us suffered had us casting our thoughts back to Ground Zero. I developed sore gums and immediately thought it was a sign of radiation. We had taken journalist Hugh Edwards with us to the site and he wrote about what we had experienced. As a result, the site was closed, which makes you wonder what would have happened if we hadn't taken along the Geiger counter and simply accepted what the authorities had told us.

Lynn and I had decided to start a family and were worried about the consequences if we had indeed been contaminated. A second look at the spectacular King George River Falls on our way back answered our concerns. It was there in one of the most romantic spots on earth that our son Dean was conceived – and he turned out just fine.

By the time Dean and his brother Adam, who is four years younger, were teenagers, they were fully qualified scuba divers. I taught them everything I had learnt in a lifetime of diving, but I must admit none of us could hold a candle to a man I met on that trip. He was simply the most amazing natural diver I had ever seen. I wanted to film a segment on the Aboriginal technique of dugong-hunting from a traditional mangrove raft. We called in to One Arm Point, north of Broome in King Sound. I asked around and was told to find a bloke named Tom Wiggan who would show us how it was done. Tom was incredible. He could dive down three metres, grab a turtle and bring it back up to the surface, and he did it with no gear at all. Not so much as a face mask, let alone flippers or goggles. It was the first time I had seen an expert Aboriginal hunter in action and he blew me away. Years later, I went back to One Arm Point and wanted to film another interview with Tom. This time I was directed to the local police

station where Tom was locked up after a domestic disturbance. When I explained what I was after, the policeman in charge simply unlocked the cell and told me to take him down the street where it was quiet.

"What if he runs away?" I asked. "He won't," said the policeman, and he was right. Tom and I went down the street, had our chat and he happily headed back to the police cells.

I'm glad to say Tom Wiggan is now something of a legend, known for his skill both as a hunter and as an artist, and he features in a display at the Australian National Maritime Museum in Sydney.

If someone like Tom or the warriors of Groote Eylandt can ever be thought of as "typical", they were indeed typical of the characters we met and the adventures we experienced as we followed in Flinders' wake. It was, without exaggeration, the trip of a lifetime, and to be able to take TV viewers with us made it even more exciting. Day after day, my expectations were exceeded. It was as if we were the only people in the world, so rare was it to see another boat. From time to time, we would pull into a settlement to buy supplies but for the most part we lived off the sea's abundance. We didn't set pots to catch mudcrabs, we just walked into the mangroves and picked them up. We speared mangrove jacks and caught barramundi. We lived a dream from dawn to sundown, day after day, and with every hour we spent in the wild it became harder and harder to return to "civilisation".

A diver, right, with snorkel approaches a coral garden. Left, again on the Solomon Islands, where fish is caught for a feast in the traditional way using a vine net.

Home port

I N 1979 OUR VOYAGE around Australia, the most unforgettable trip of my life, came to an end. Heading home and simply taking up where we had left off was never going to be easy. Months of living on a boat, surviving on what we could catch or spear and knowing the pleasures of total freedom, made the thought of returning to our home on the Gold Coast less than attractive.

Over the years, because of the success of my work, I had been able to achieve what I thought of as the Great Australian Dream. I had a house on the riverfront at Paradise Waters, with my boat moored out the back on my own jetty. It was the sort of home base that people aspire to all their lives. Yet coming back from our journey I knew it was no longer for me. The Gold Coast had become a concrete jungle. High-rise buildings blocked out the sun, the streets were full of tacky souvenir shops and a rough element had arrived, attracted by nightclubs and the drug scene. Lynn and I knew it wasn't where we wanted to live and raise a family. As we cruised down the coast in *Beva*, we decided we would look for a new place to live. Whenever we docked, we would be thinking: "Is this the place for us?" But nothing really seemed to jump out at us. Until …

One day we sailed into Port Douglas. I looked around for somewhere to moor and saw an old wharf at an abandoned and dilapidated sugar-storage shed. I tied up, took a quick look at the building and said to Lynn, "This is it!" I had found my dream home.

Lynn didn't exactly share my enthusiasm first off. She looked at the old timber shed, which was partly falling down and had holes in the roof and walls, and she saw, well, an old shed. I saw much more and, to Lynn's credit, she backed me all the way.

 *My Shipwreck Museum at Port Douglas.*

Over the years, my home at Paradise Waters had begun to overflow with all the artefacts and relics I had collected on my treasure-hunting expeditions. What had started as a few pots and old jars on a shelf or two inside the house had become a double garage packed with everything from cannon balls to brass alarm clocks and giant anchors. The relics stayed safe and dry inside under lock and key while my car was outside on the street at the mercy of the elements.

The more I collected, the more my vision of a shipwreck museum became clearer. When I saw the old wharf and warehouse at Port Douglas all the pieces fell into place. I could create my museum in the front of the building and we could live at the back, literally hanging over the water. It was perfect. All I had to do was get my hands on it.

Port Douglas back in 1979 was still a sleepy village with no footpaths, no upmarket boutiques and no art galleries, let alone any five-star tourist resorts. Now houses with water views regularly change hands for millions of dollars, but when Lynn and I tied up *Beva* on that wharf no-one living there thought of "Port" as a potential goldmine; it was just their own little piece of paradise.

After seeing as much of the wharf and shed as I could, and being further convinced that it was exactly what we were looking for, my first step was to hitch a ride inland to the town of Mossman, and head for the offices of Douglas Shire Council.

As the property was Crown land on the harbour foreshore, it came under the auspices of the Queensland government. It could not be bought, or even rented, but it could be leased. As with all properties of this kind, the responsibility for its upkeep and management lay with the local council, in this case Douglas Shire. It didn't take much of a look to realise that this property wasn't high on the shire's list of priorities. Douglas Shire was largely made up of farming communities and, as such, its councillors were more interested in the harvesting of sugar cane and pineapples than in abandoned wharves. When I asked them their plans for the building,

Shark hunters bring their kill to the boat.

the answer was that they didn't see a future for it at all. They planned to demolish it at some stage, if nature didn't do the job for them first. Having negotiated with Hollywood producers as well as tiger sharks, I can be pretty persuasive when I want to be. I convinced the councillors that this was a building of great historic and aesthetic value, which needed to be saved. What really sold them was my plan for a Shipwreck Museum. Port Douglas was a beautiful spot, but the tourist industry had yet to reach that far north. I said if they agreed to renovate the building I would certainly be one of the first to put in a tender to lease it.

They agreed and I was good to my word. In fact, I was the only tenderer. Obviously no-one else could see what I saw, and I was able to sign a 20-year lease at a weekly rent of $100. It might seem a pittance now, but back in 1979 it wasn't cheap, particularly when you consider that I was responsible for all repairs, maintenance and upkeep.

When the lease was signed and the council renovations complete, we set about planning alterations to make the building suitable for our needs. I found out that the wharf and shed had been built in 1906 to service the big ships that carried the sugar cane south to the refineries. It had obviously been built well because it was one of the few buildings to survive a cyclone in 1911 that destroyed most of the town. Newspaper clippings I found reported that many townspeople had sheltered there during the storm. I didn't have as much faith as them. Whenever we got a bad cyclone warning, I would move my family somewhere safer for fear the shed would blow away.

While we headed to the Solomon Islands to film a TV series, a builder friend, Jack Anderson, fitted out the shed to our specifications. By Christmas 1980, Lynn and I and our one-year-old Dean were able to move into our home over the water.

It really was a beautiful spot, this big white timber building sticking right out over the water, and once we got things the way we wanted

My boat Beva *(named originally for Ben and Eva) moored alongside my wharf home at Port Douglas.*

them, it was the only place I wanted to live. It might have been a shed on the outside, but to us it was home. It was such an unusual property that it featured in a pictorial spread in House & Garden magazine. There we lived, close by all the things we loved: the Great Barrier Reef, the rainforest, the mangroves and of course the water lapping beneath us. I could fish from the wharf or just slip down with my speargun to shoot any barramundi I fancied for dinner. We had crab-pots and could catch bait for taking out on the boat. It was heaven.

Sadly, Port Douglas was a secret too good to keep. As word of our little village spread and the road from Cairns was widened and improved, it was inevitable the developers and trendies would follow. When we first moved in, Port was just a sleepy little village with a great harbour, a couple of very good restaurants and 300 community-minded residents. Everyone knew everyone else and when you walked up the street everyone waved and said gidday.

Across the road from our home was an excellent restaurant named Catalina. We would eat there often, walking in barefoot and sitting down for a meal with our little dog, Tuffy, lying at our feet under the table. I also remember walking out of my front door to the park next door and picking up delicious mangos, which had fallen from the trees and were lying on the grass.

I finally opened my museum in 1981 after trucking my relics up from the Gold Coast. It proved a great success and became a Port Douglas landmark. The museum was never intended as a money-making venture. I purposely kept the admission prices low, especially for children, because I wanted as many people as possible to have the chance to learn about our seafaring heritage. As long I broke even, I was satisfied.

Port, as the locals call it, proved to be a wonderful place to raise our two boys, very much like my own upbringing at Lennox Head. It was a bit scary when they were young – we had to be very watchful in case they fell in the water. They never did, although I had to rescue the cat and dog a couple of times. We taught the boys to swim very early and from then

Solomon Islanders
haul a whaler shark
aboard their boat.
Photo by Lynn Cropp.

on they had a ball. They were always doing something active outside: swimming, wakeboard-riding, diving. There was no going to the mall to play video machines or sitting around on the Internet. I think it would be hard to grow up a bad person in an environment like that.

Our home base at Port Douglas was the perfect starting point for my expeditions, but it didn't take me long to realise that I could do a lot of filming right off our wharf, without even leaving home. I filmed deadly box jellyfish and crocodiles. I remember one time looking out the kitchen window and seeing a crocodile on the surface near the little beach where we used to swim with the boys. Another time I told the boys not to jump off the wharf because I had seen a crocodile hanging around. They weren't too happy about it, but they stopped their game. The next day we saw the croc sitting on the opposite bank just watching the boys.

But it wasn't natural predators that finally forced us from our home. It was progress and greed. I admit I bought quite a bit of property in Port Douglas and sold it for a profit over the years, but making money was never the reason I lived there. I would honestly much prefer never to have made a cent and to have Port back the way it was when I first saw it. I know I'm not the only one.

In 1999 my lease ended and the property came up for tender. This was a different Douglas Shire Council from the one I had addressed 20 years earlier. By now the tourism dollar and property speculation were far more important to councillors than farm productivity and rainfall. It was all about the bottom line and the council envisaged raking in a very high rental for the wharf and shed. There were a number of remarks from councillors in the press that I had "privatised" the property by living there with my family.

The fact that the building housed the museum, one of the last links to the old Port Douglas, didn't come into their thinking. Neither did they seem to remember that if it hadn't been for me they would have allowed the shed to fall into the sea. I knew I had no chance when the mayor was

The manta ray, the largest species of ray in the world, can reach up to 6.7m wide.

quoted along the lines of "Ben has the best spot in Port Douglas; why should he be allowed to live there?"

Still, I put in my tender based on what I could afford, which I knew would be a long way from what they expected. I was right. Once again I was the only tenderer. No-one else was silly enough to consider putting their money into a wonky old building needing regular, and costly, upkeep. Nevertheless, the council would not accept my tender and decided to retain the wharf for public use. As far as finding a new home was concerned, much as it was sad to leave, it wasn't devastating. The reality is that living in a leased property is always a risk. Once the lease is up there are no guarantees. As it turned out I was able to lease another property on the harbourfront and moor my boat on my own wharf just as before.

Being forced to close down the museum was heartbreaking. To me, a museum should be forever, not just a place that lives or dies at the whim of bureaucrats. It was never about money, always about giving people access to treasures they would never have the chance to see otherwise. I also felt I was giving something back to the community which had embraced my family 20 years earlier. Once I opened the museum I felt I had a moral obligation to keep it going, no matter how much it cost me. Unfortunately, the councillors didn't share my view. Port Douglas had become a money-making machine and the mighty dollar was all that mattered. Four years on, the building remains empty and my museum pieces sit in storage.

I couldn't count the number of people in the years since who have told me how much they miss that museum. Singer John Farnham, who holidayed regularly in Port Douglas with his family, and spent time on our boat, says that every time he passes the empty building he feels like crying. I know just how he feels.

Family adventures

TO PARAPHRASE the old adage: you can pick your shipmates, but you can't pick your family. How lucky does that make me then, because in my case they have often been one and the same.

I was reluctant to start a family. Call it selfish if you like, but I felt my way of life was not conducive to having children. My ambition had always been to be like Hans Hass who sailed the world with his wife, Lotte. I didn't see Hans and Lotte nursing young children, changing nappies or warming bottles as they explored exotic locations and I couldn't see how I could manage it either. As much as it might seem I was only thinking of myself, I was also well aware that it would not be fair to leave my wife behind with our children as I lived the life of a seafaring nomad.

When Lynn gave birth to Dean in 1980, my attitudes changed. Once I held my son for the first time any worries I might have had went straight out the window, and as for any concerns about the detrimental effect children might have on my career, it turned out to be quite the opposite. With the birth of Dean, and of Adam four years later, I went from a latter-day buccaneer making films of his adventures to a family man taking his wife and children around Australia with him. Suddenly my films were attracting a whole new audience. While the early films showed me doing things that most people couldn't dream of, the later films were more accessible to ordinary people. Families could watch them together and put themselves in our place. They could relate because they could see a real family, just like their own, doing amazing things. And it wasn't just the boys. We also took along our family pets, Scruffy the silky terrier and Streaker the cat. There was nothing "put on" about it, that was just our family, living the way we lived.

Scruffy taught me a good lesson about the appeal of being ourselves. The first time I took him on a filming trip he kept running in and out of

Catching mudcrabs to survive as a family for seven days while "marooned" on Forbes Island to make Survival on a Coral Isle. *Photo by Lynn Cropp.*

picture and yapping. He was just that kind of dog; he wanted to be in the middle of whatever was happening. For the first half of the trip I kept shoo-ing him away or locking him up so his barking didn't wreck the sound recording. After a while I thought: "This is ridiculous. He is part of the crew, and if he gets in the shot then that's just the way it is." Pretty soon Scruffy started getting fan mail and wherever I went people asked about him. It seemed as if I had set out to make a film about tiger sharks and ended up making *Scruffy Goes to Sea*. Scruffy starred in several of my films and people still remember the film of him swimming and playing with the dolphins at Monkey Mia. He led a charmed existence – I must have saved his life at least three of four times. His problem was that he didn't know he was a dog. He thought that anything I could do, he could do just as well. He'd seen me fishing all his life so he figured it was a perfectly normal thing for a dog to emulate. His technique was to walk into the shallows and snap away at anything that moved. Hardly surprisingly Scruffy met with limited success, but one time his love of fishing almost saw him the hunted instead of the hunter. During a trip to the Kimberleys Scruffy was doing his thing in shallow water when a pack of whaler sharks headed towards him. I had to run down the beach and throw rocks at them as he reluctantly made his retreat. One of Scruffy's tricks was to pick up in his mouth any fish I pulled on board our boat. Once he grabbed a giant mackerel by the tail and the fish flicked him straight over the side. I had to turn the boat around to pick him up. Then there was the time he was walking along a beach with me when a wedge-tail eagle tried to pick him up and fly off. Somehow Scruffy managed to survive it all and live a long and full life, as did my next terrier, Tuffy, and my latest, Tuffy II.

Streaker the cat also loved fish, but he was a lot more careful than Scruffy. Streaker only ever fell in the water once. He became quite a star in my films and even did a TV ad for Whiskas cat food, and when he died, he earned an obituary in a newspaper. People used to write to me saying they felt as if Streaker were part of their family.

It was the same with the boys. People loved to see them grow a little bigger and more capable with each film. Lynn and I took them with us on every expedition that *Beva* made. Living the lives they did, it was very important to teach them to swim as early as possible. I had learned that

My terrier Scruffy swims after dolphins at Monkey Mia, in WA, in 1978. Photo by Lynn Cropp.

the quickest way to teach someone to swim was to put flippers and a face mask on them and then, when they are confident in the water, take them off. Both our boys could swim almost before they could walk, but that didn't mean we could take our eyes off them. We watched them constantly and, considering the situations we found ourselves in, there were very few scrapes. It was only in their teenage years, when they were experienced divers and perhaps a little over-confident, that they pushed their luck when fooling around with sharks.

Once, we were in a rubber dinghy filming tiger sharks attacking a dead turtle that we had found on a beach. The turtle was secured on a buoy we were pulling off the back of the dinghy. It seemed fine at the time – we had done it dozens of times before – but on this occasion three sharks lost interest in the turtle and came in very close to the dinghy. The moment passed and none of us gave it too much thought. It wasn't until years later when a tiger shark tore apart a dinghy I was in that I remembered that day with my boys and realised the risk we had taken. It gave me a cold shiver down my spine to think about it. It still does.

Probably the hairiest moment we had during that period didn't involve the boys or Lynn at all, but rather it was me who ended up in difficulties. We were white-water rafting south of Cairns after being dropped by helicopter at the top of South Johnson River. It was a wild ride; one second I was filming and the next I was fighting for my life. I was sucked under the water and pushed against a boulder. Although I was wearing a life vest, I was under water for a minute. I had to claw my way back up the side of the rock using both hands and finished with cuts and bruises and nothing else to show for it. I never saw that camera again.

The dangers of the deep weren't really what our family adventure films were about. They were aimed at a younger, broader audience, particularly families, which was why the Disney organisation bought so many and why I spent so much time researching and looking for unusual experiences we could share on film. Whether it was reading newspapers or magazines or simply hearing some old-timer talk of something he had seen or heard, I was always on the look-out for something, which would make a film – and an unforgettable trip for the Cropp family.

It all added up to a great life for the boys. They packed more adventures into their first few years than most people do in a lifetime.

 *A seal and a diver in the Galapagos islands.*

When Dean was 10 and Adam six, they starred in their own film, *Young Adventurers*, which was nominated for an Emmy award after it was shown on the Disney Channel. Earlier still, when Dean was just a baby we took him with us when we sailed to the Solomon Islands. The Islanders loved his blond hair and would play with him on the boat for hours. We took a babysitter with us on that trip, but she got plenty of help. When Dean and Adam were 15 and 11, we made an updated version of *Young Adventurers*, called Adventures of the Cropp Family. By then, both boys had their advanced scuba tickets and were as capable as most professional divers. In that film, I took them down 30 metres to the wreck of the *Pandora*.

During another family outing, we went diving with giant whale sharks near Ningaloo Reef off the North West Cape of Western Australia. Spotter planes located the sharks for us and, on an average day, we would swim with three of the gentle giants. There is nothing more exhilarating in diving than coming face to face with a 10-metre shark, its 1.5 metre jaws open to feed as it glides past. Further down the WA coast at Cape Cuvier, we witnessed the greatest feeding frenzy I had ever seen as some 200 whaler sharks and two bryde's whales corralled a massive school of pilchards and plunged into them.

One adventure that Lynn and I enjoyed, but the boys, then 12 and eight, weren't so enthusiastic about, was when I decided to make a film on how to survive for a week if shipwrecked on a coral island. We went through the whole process, from getting to the beach on a liferaft to catching or foraging for everything we ate. Coconuts were our main diet, but climbing the trees to get them proved a lot harder than it looks. We made spears to catch fish and I speared a 10-kilo trevally by standing near the bait fish and waiting for it to go for the bait. It was interesting to see that even kids like mine who were used to an outdoors lifestyle found it difficult to live without some home comforts. Adam complained of being hungry and when we asked the boys at the end of the week what they missed most, they answered immediately: "TV and milkshakes." Gee, and I thought the drink I'd made by mixing green ants with water was just as nice.

Of all the films we made as a family, two stand out, *Secrets of the Billabong* and *March of the Crabs*.

For Secrets of the Billabong we chose remote Lake Polly in Lakefield National Park near Cooktown. It was isolated, unspoilt and had lots of wildlife. We could walk along the lake at dawn and there would be freshwater crocodiles sitting on the bank. The boys were really the stars of

"The old man of the sea" heads home in his dinghy after a dive; Dean was just eight when he caught this nice "red".

the film because we had footage of them doing things like nursing a lost joey and fishing for barramundi. It was all lovely, feel-good kids-in-the-wild stuff. What we didn't show was all the behind-the-scenes footage taken at the start of the trip, which we could have packaged under the title *The Family Holiday From Hell*.

Lake Polly was so remote and the track so hard to follow that as we drove through the bush in our four-wheel-drive we had to stop and tie toilet paper around the trees so we could find our way back out. When we arrived, the boys were keen to go fishing for barramundi so I told them to head down to the water while I got the camera. Obviously the barra at Lake Polly weren't used to seeing fishing lures because before I had my camera ready, Dean had thrown his line out and landed a nice big one. I wanted to get it off the hook quickly so I could film him catching another one, but as I pulled the hook out the fish flipped and put the hook right through my thumb. I got the pliers to pull it out, but couldn't manage it. There was only one thing to do. We hadn't even unpacked, but it was back into the truck for the 40-kilometre drive back to the ranger station. Lynn had to drive the whole way, following the toilet paper trail, because I had the lure sticking out of my thumb.

When we got there the ranger took one look and said I had a choice: either he could call the Flying Doctor, which would mean a wait of a few hours, followed by an overnight stay in hospital, or, as he said, "I'll yank it out in five minutes using my secret method." I opted for the second option on condition he gave me a beer first.

The ranger's "secret method" entailed pulling the hook out against the barb. He got a piece of string which he tied as close to the barb as possible, told me to hold my thumb as tightly as I could with my other hand and yanked on the string with all his strength. The hook came straight out. We got into the truck again and followed the toilet paper trail back to the lake – and had a puncture halfway. Finally back at our campsite, we unpacked for a wonderful three-week stay. And yes, the barra were waiting.

The other film I remember so well was also the most successful I ever made in terms of international sales and public reaction. Ask people today which of my films they remember most and, more times than not, they will say: "that one with all the crabs".

The March of the Crabs project began, like many of my films, as I was flicking through a magazine, and photos and an accompanying article sparked my attention. The writer described the annual pilgrimage of 80 million red crabs as they march down the mountains of Christmas

The Cropp family in 1991, from left, Dean, me with Tuffy, Adam and Lynn. Efficient fishermen from an early age, Dean and Adam display two fine barramundi caught for dinner.

Island to the waters of the Indian Ocean to spawn. It seemed too extraordinary to be true, but when I tracked down the photographer he assured me it was just as the article said, 80 million crabs heading to the beach at midnight. I immediately started making plans to be there for the next march. The film was pre-sold to my usual distributors and I pinpointed the time for the migration as best I could. I read everything I could find about the march of the crabs and felt I was pretty much up to speed on what I would be filming, but nothing could prepare me for what awaited us on Christmas Island.

We had rented a cottage near the beach and waited for the march to start. What we weren't prepared for was the "advance party". As a filmmaker, I could never have scripted what nature had created.

It was an incredible story. There were about 14,000 red crabs to the hectare on the island, living off fallen leaves and seeds from chestnut trees. For 10 months of the year, they lived quietly in burrows, but in November when the first monsoon rains arrived they began their eight-kilometre, two-week trek to the sea. The males moved first, the females followed, and little by little the crabs began to invade the modern world. It was not a sympathetic environment. Before they could reach the sea, about two million crabs would be killed, mostly when crossing roads. For the human inhabitants of Christmas Island, the pilgrimage brought its own challenges. Walking or going for a jog along footpaths teeming with crabs, finding cupboards, drawers or washing machines invaded by little red visitors – even playing golf when hundreds of crabs had set up camp on the putting green – it all made life interesting to say the least.

For my purposes, the assistance of Dean and Adam proved invaluable, and not just because by now they were extremely competent cameramen taking their own footage for inclusion in the film. Rather, their natural reaction to the amazing phenomenon they were experiencing made this the ultimate Cropp family adventure. The crabs would crawl over the boys' beds as they tried to get to sleep, attempt to drag their sandals outside and, if they didn't remember to shut the door firmly, they would find themselves showering with several visitors.

Runners try to avoid a mass of red crabs on the roadway at Christmas Island during the crabs' annual migration to the sea for breeding.

All this was captured on film, as were other stunning examples of Christmas Island wildlife, but it was the night of the spawning that we filmed which was an unforgettable natural wonder.

One afternoon we noticed thousands of crabs heading to the foreshore and taking up their positions. This would be the night. That evening we headed to the beach and looked up at the cliff face to see it had turned red as millions of female crabs jockeyed for the best spot from which to drop their eggs into the sea for hatching. By midnight, the entire foreshore was covered by tens of millions, and at 1 am as the tide came in, the crabs started jerking and shaking their eggs into the surf. It was like a storm, clumps of eggs falling from the cliff face and turning the water grey.

As the tide began to recede, the females poured down the cliff face and swarmed onto the beach to chase the retreating waters. It was then I got the shot that so many people remember. Dean was kneeling on the sand filming, and the lamp on his camera attracted the crabs. He found himself becoming more and more buried under a pile of crabs, a few hundred at first, then a thousand or so and finally 10 times that many, as the crabs climbed 20 deep over him. When he stood up, the crabs clung to him. Shining his light towards the sea, he shuffled into the water like the Pied Piper, taking thousands of hitch-hikers with him.

The red crab eggs hatched immediately they came into contact with the water and were swept out to sea as their mothers headed back up the mountain, running the same gamut of car tyres and golf balls on the way. The billions of hatched eggs had their own predators to survive, most serious among them the whale sharks, which time their visit to Christmas Island to coincide with the red crab spawn. Four weeks later, the surviving young crabs returned to the beach and began their own odyssey to the mountains.

To see this amazing spectacle and share it with my sons was a special experience. It probably epitomises what that period of our lives was all about, the Cropp family adventuring and taking it to the world. Some people might say it was a strange upbringing for two boys. I say it was a wonderful upbringing. They could snorkel when they were four years old, scuba dive just a few years later. They knew how to handle spearguns, fishing rods or movie cameras as well as any professional three times their

Dean films a mass of spawning red crabs on the island.

209

Giants of the seas:
A humpback whale
dives off Fraser Island
(photo by Lynn Cropp)
and an enormous
clam attracts a diver.

age and they gained an understanding and appreciation of nature that all young men could well do with. Everything they learned in their early years has stood them in good stead. Adam is a professional diver with Sea World, often involved in helping injured or stranded marine creatures, while Dean is a news cameraman, still living a life of adventure filming out of helicopters, being sent to war zones around the world, and filming underwater news stories.

And there is another thing my sons still do. Every year, without fail, when I get ready to make my latest film I don't have to think about who I'll take along as my assistants. Just as in the days of *Beva*, they don't let me go without them.

Run aground

Adam practises survival on Forbes Island, Qld. Below, Lynn feeds the friendly dolphins of Monkey Mia in 1978.

MY MARRIAGE and my boat ran aground on the same night. My 48-foot Grand Banks vessel *Beva* was the most well-known ship in Australia, thanks to the power of television. When Eva left me and I married Lynn, *Beva* became a special part of our lives. It featured in more than 20 documentaries and, for 11 years, it was the focus of my professional and personal life.

The day of New Year's Eve 1985 was an absolute scorcher, the hottest in Far North Queensland in years. There was a strong wind warning from

the north-west so I decided to anchor *Beva* on the seaward south side of Low Isles off Port Douglas, where I felt we would be sheltered. Lynn and I took the boys along, thinking it would be a pleasant way to see in the New Year. We tied up on the big Quicksilver mooring, had dinner and put the boys to bed, then sat down to enjoy a relaxed evening.

About 10 pm the wind began to scream around us, coming hard from the south at more than 60 knots. I remember looking up at the clear sky full of stars and wondering what was causing the big blow. It certainly wasn't a regular cyclone.

The movie *A Perfect Storm* explained how certain elements must all come into play at precisely the same time to create a giant storm. That is what happened that night. The storm we were caught in was a dry windstorm, or tornado. It had been created when the land cooled rapidly that night after the record temperatures of the day. The sea temperature, however, stayed constant. In effect, a high pressure built up over the land and a low pressure over the sea. The wind raced down the coastal mountains to the sea to fill the gap in pressure and my family, aboard *Beva*, was slap-bang in its path.

As we were tethered to the big mooring I was not unduly worried, believing we could ride out the storm. What I didn't know was that the mooring was badly placed for a southerly, and *Beva*'s stern was above a protruding coral bommie.

The swell lifted the boat and dumped the stern straight onto the coral. I shouted to Lynn over the roaring wind to go down to the main bedroom to check on Adam, who was 18 months old. She found him asleep in his cot, with water swirling around him. On impact, the coral had stoved the rudder through the hull. Lynn picked up Adam and tied him to her waist with a piece of rope, and I tried without success to stop the water pouring in through the hole. With the boat beginning to list badly, I made my way to the radio and put out a Mayday call, knowing full well it would be hours before anyone could reach us because of the huge seas.

I grabbed five-year-old Dean in my arms and, together with Lynn and Adam, we climbed back on deck. As the boat slipped further on its side, all we could do was cling to a rail on the aft deck with waves breaking over us. We tried to keep Streaker the cat and Tuffy the dog close to us lest they were washed over the side, but that was only one of my concerns. Directly

 *The perfect storm builds beyond a coral cay.*

across the deck from where we huddled was a heavy cabinet holding the Scuba compressor. With each movement of the boat, the risk of the cabinet sliding across the deck became greater. With difficulty, I got Lynn and the boys to a safer spot. Minutes later, the cabinet came loose and rolled across the deck, smashing against the railing where we had been. It would have crushed us all.

For hours, we crouched on the deck, clutching our children as the storm blew itself out. Finally, in the early hours of the morning, we were rescued and taken by boat to Low Isles. As soon as we stepped on dry land, Streaker lived up to his name and headed for the bush. It took us four days to find him. As for me, I sat on the sand and cried at the loss of my beloved boat.

That stormy night proved to be a turning point for all of us. *Beva* was replaced – first by the 52-foot cruiser *Call of the Wild*; then in 1989 by the catamaran cruiser *Freedom*; and then by *Freedom II* and my present cat cruiser *Freedom III* – but nothing would ever be the same again.

The boys were not emotionally scarred – they would come on many adventures with me over the ensuing years – but Lynn could never again feel the same way about the sea. If the wind reached 20 knots, she would start shaking as memories of that night came back. She could not bring herself to head off on a long voyage again. As it was the way I made my living, I was forced to sail off alone, sometimes for months at a time. That storm became the catalyst for the breakdown of our happy marriage.

Ironically, in time I would add pieces salvaged from *Beva* to others I had on display in the Shipwreck Museum. As someone who had spent years searching for wrecks and tracing the memoirs of survivors, I now knew first-hand how it felt to see the most valuable things in your life break up against a coral reef.

On so many levels, it hurt.

Lynn with the anchor of an old sailing ship we discovered at Great Detached Reef.

Second time around

FROM THE MOMENT I had dropped anchor after our voyage around Australia, I dreamed of going back to the Kimberley coast. It took me 20 years, but in 1996 I was finally able to put together a second expedition to some of the most spectacular landscapes I had ever seen. Once again, the trip was financed by Channel Seven, which ordered a series of three adventure films, one each on Cape York, the Wild North of Arnhem Land and the Kimberley coast.

This time I took a full crew, including three cameramen, to ensure that we didn't miss anything that happened, and believe me, a lot did. The crew comprised my sons and me as cameramen; a young English woman named Jacquie King, who was attractive and animated on camera; Hoss Saunders, a cousin of ours; Michelle Mason; Sarina Delanis and a young man named Nick Schlipper. Nick was an action man. Very fit and athletic, he was one of those characters who would try anything, especially if there were a camera nearby. If I needed someone to climb a tree, swing across a creek on a rope or throw a mud ball at a croc to see if it was awake, Nick was my man. As always, I put a lot of thought into the make-up of the team. Living in close quarters required a certain harmony, but at the same time this wasn't a holiday. We were making a movie and there had to be a definite chemistry to make the film come alive. In a way, I was trying to replicate the family feel of the movies I had made with Lynn and the boys when they were younger, and on this trip I got the mix right. The crew were an eager and high-spirited group, which, given what I had in store for them, was just as well.

Our first expedition was to walk to the top of Hunter Creek on the eastern side of Cape York Peninsula. I had flown over the area years earlier and been amazed at what I saw. The creek came to a magnificent red gorge where it spilled over in twin waterfalls. It looked like the sort of landscape one would see in the Kimberleys rather than Cape York Peninsula, so I had

The magic of the Kimberleys in WA ... the breathtaking King George River Falls.

always wanted to go back for a closer look. My interest was further flamed because, much as I asked around, I could not find anyone who had been there. I told Dick Smith about it in the hope he could fly his helicopter down into the gorge, but the sheer size of the waterfalls made it impossible. There was only one way in, and that was on foot.

The journey proved a lot harder than I had envisaged. On the map, the distance from the mouth of the creek, where we moored our boat, to the falls looked to be five kilometres, but creeks don't run in a straight line. What I thought was five kilometres turned out to be 25 kilometres – and a tough 25 kilometres at that.

We set off at dawn, carrying my trusty dinghy across a sandhill, then we paddled across the salt-water part of the creek until we came to a rock bar blocking our way. The only way to continue was to leave the dinghy and walk up the centre of the creek. It was a slow and uncomfortable trip, with the water sometimes up to our shoulders. With the camera boxes balanced on our heads to keep dry, we looked like a safari scene from an old Tarzan movie. We assumed there were no fresh-water crocodiles around because of the number of rock bars, until one slid into the water nearby. Knowing fresh-water crocs are not usually aggressive, we waded past, never taking our eyes off him for a second.

It took us six hours to reach the gorge, but once we saw the stunning, giant red cliffs with water tumbling 75 metres from the plateau above, any physical discomfort was irrelevant. What made the sight even more spectacular was that it was totally out of character for the area. We felt as if we had discovered one of the last unexplored parts of Australia and I have no doubt we were the first non-Aboriginal people to stand before this incredible work of nature. Given that the only way in or out was to wade along the creek, I doubt anyone else would have even contemplated the trip. This was a nice thought, but the prospect of another six-hour trek back to the dinghy wasn't quite as appealing.

The return trip was one of the most physically demanding I have ever undertaken. A few years later, I would trek the Inca trail in South America, but this was its equal. Halfway back, I was like a zombie, plodding along slowly, barely able to put one foot in front of the other. Thankfully, with a few hours still to go, I got my second wind and was able to stride out more comfortably, but there were times when I wondered if I would make

My boat Freedom III, *the latest in a long line of vessels I've owned. Photo by John Harding.*

it back. When I reached the dinghy, I noticed my sons, more than 40 years my junior, flaked out on the sand, and that made me feel a little better. Memories of the pain have long faded, but my appreciation of the sight which met us when we emerged from the scrub never will. I would gladly go back, but next time I would take more supplies and spend more time exploring and savouring the spectacle. It is one place I have been which I am confident will not have changed over the years.

From Cape York, we continued further into the Gulf name TK and, as always, fished for barramundi up the rivers as we went. It was on one of our daily fishing stops that Dean cast his lure into a tree. Instead of jerking the rod sideways to free it, he yanked it straight back and the lure hooked itself into Adam's knee. It is times like that when I find myself torn between my compassion as a father and my professionalism as a cameraman. Needless to say, I kept filming, much to Adam's annoyance.

"Dad," he yelled between cries of pain. "Don't film this."

"I have to," I said. "Last time this happened the hook was in me and I missed the shot. I'm not going to miss this one." I also told him it was a good opportunity for me to try that secret method of hook removal the ranger had showed us back at Lake Polly. The ranger was right. It worked.

The hook in Adam's knee was the first of a series of injuries that struck us en route. Adam liked to think it was karma for me filming him in his moment of pain, the final injury score being Adam, 1, Ben, 3. First I tripped over a log when filming and, in trying to protect the camera, managed to hurt my back. Then there was the big box jellyfish I picked up and mishandled, allowing it to slide down my arm spreading poison as it went, and finally came the injury I sustained while filming a second "trial by spear".

I wanted to re-film the traditional ceremony on Groote Eylandt 20 years on, but the Umbakumba people we encountered the second time around were very different from those we had met earlier. The local policeman who had been so helpful in 1978 was long gone and trying to organise the tribesmen myself was no easy thing. Where once there had been great enthusiasm and excitement at the thought of demonstrating their traditional skills, there was now apathy. Whether there had been a change of attitude at the settlement or the townspeople were intimidated

This three-metre saltwater crocodile swam out from shore at Port Essington, NT, to circle my boat for an hour.

by the number of cameras I was now using, I'm not sure, but it was certainly a different experience. No-one asked for money, but I gave out videos of the previous filming and made a donation to the community in the hope of stirring up some enthusiasm. In the end it took hours and hours of pleading, cajoling and threats by the head man to convince the warriors to take part. The first time we had filmed at Groote Eylandt there was virtually a public holiday to allow everyone from school kids to elders to watch, with hundreds enjoying the spectacle. This time there were no spectators, just 10 men who reluctantly showed up to take part.

Once again, padded caps were placed over the tips of the spears and one man volunteered to be the victim, dancing around to avoid the spears. My action man, Nick, asked if he could take part and the tribesmen agreed, making him a spear and even giving him an Aboriginal name, Wongaling. I'm not sure what it meant, perhaps something like "clumsy white man who hits boss with throwing stick" because, as I filmed Nick in action, I got too close and he followed through with his Woomera (throwing stick) and smashed me on the shin. It was the only blood spilt in the whole fight.

After allowing Nick to be a spear thrower, the Aborigines decided he should also take a turn as the victim. Never one to refuse a challenge, Nick jumped at the chance – literally. Because he was so fit and agile, he managed to avoid being hit, which annoyed the throwers no end. A few got together and threw their spears at once, but Nick still jumped out of the way. Finally, all 10 warriors rushed at him en masse and he took off with them in hot pursuit. They chased him into the water where one scored

A crocodile makes short work of a pig. And, above, I lie in the mud to film mudskippers in the mangroves for a TV film. Lyn took both photos.

a hit to much hilarity. Nick and I limped off, with the Umbakumba men obviously enjoying the experience a lot more at the end than they had at the beginning.

From Groote Eylandt we continued on to Arnhem Land to see what we could see. There was nothing scripted about the film we made, no set-up shots. We simply set off into the unknown and filmed whatever turned up. The wildlife was so abundant that there was always something worth filming, especially in the clear waters of Arnhem Land. One day we sailed into Port Essington to shoot some footage of the old settlement there. We were off the point when we spotted several manta-rays so we cut the motor and filmed them drifting alongside the boat, clearly visible in the water. Soon another interested onlooker, a three-metre crocodile, joined us, swimming out from the shore to see what all the commotion was about. The crocodile swam around the boat looking at us. The water was so clear that we could see every detail. It was the most beautiful film I ever took of a croc swimming. He never took his beady eyes off us as he circled our boat for an hour.

As keen barramundi hunters, we encountered plenty of crocodiles. There's an old fishermen's saying: "Where there's crocs, there's barras." A crocodile's main diet is catfish, which eat the spawn of barramundi, so a crocodile is always a good sign when you are looking for a barra hole. During that trip we followed the crocs to what looked like a good fishing spot at the mouth of a creek. It was a great spot, but it wasn't crocodiles we had to worry about that day, it was sharks. The fish were really biting, but we lost half our catch to a pack of small whaler sharks that were literally fighting each other – and us – to get the hooked fish. One of the sharks got caught on the lure that had hooked the fish it was trying to snatch. The other sharks were also trying to grab the same fish and the hooked shark leapt two metres in the air to free itself. It was the only time I have ever seen a shark jump out of the water, and we got it on film.

When we arrived in the Kimberleys, Adam, Nick and I paddled out in the dinghy to cast for barra while Dean fished on the bank. As we fished from the dinghy, Adam saw what he thought was a rock – until it disappeared, and he realised it was a three-metre crocodile. When the croc surfaced, he kept his eye on it. We heard Dean call out, "I've got a good one", and Adam saw the croc turn and head straight for the fish Dean

Another view of the three-metre saltie that took a particular interest in my boat off Port Essington, NT.

The underwater filmmaker ready for work. Right, the falls at the end of the King George River gorge in WA make it the most scenic place I know.

was pulling in. "Look out, Dean," we yelled, "Croc!" Dean was up and running in a second – not away from the water as I'd expected, but into it. He waded in, grabbed the fish and pulled it up onto the rocks. "He's not getting my barra," he shouted back to us.

The crocodile stuck around and grabbed Adam's lure. Instinctively, Adam started playing the three-metre croc on his six-kilo line, as he would a big fish. As I filmed, Adam brought the croc under the dinghy and then, carried away in the heat of the battle, started pulling it up to our inflatable dinghy. Luckily, Nick had a sudden rush of clear-headedness, reached over and broke the line. That was one of dozens of lures we lost on the trip for one reason or another. When we ran out completely, Nick experimented with some empty .303 cartridges. He drilled holes in them and inserted a trace and hook, and they worked a treat. In wild areas, fish will go for anything. I've seen a bloke tie a hook on a clothes peg and catch a good-sized barra. When they are really biting, anything does.

Dean taking on that croc to get his fish and Adam almost pulling the same croc into the dinghy shows how over-confident and blasé we had become around crocodiles, just as we were around sharks. It took 20 years for a tiger shark to almost get the better of me in that same dinghy. Looking back now, we were lucky not to get into similar strife with a croc.

Soon after the fishing incident, we headed to a creek that I knew had been a major spot for crocodile hunters back in the days before shooting crocs was banned. It was almost a breeding place for them, and I had been told that 4,000 had been shot there over a three-year period. By the time we arrived, the population had grown back to previous numbers. Perhaps foolishly, we set out in the dinghy to do some filming. We saw a crocodile lying on the bank, covered in mud. Jacquie, who had obviously done some research before the trip, told us this was to prevent skin cancer, which I had never heard before. The croc slipped into the water and floated in front of the dinghy as we filmed. Hoss was driving and Jacquie wasn't impressed. "Hoss, you're going too close, you're too close," she was saying fearfully. I got better footage of her than I did of the croc.

It was up one of those creeks that I saw the largest crocodile I have ever seen. As we cruised along, it took fright and leapt off the bank into the water. I would estimate it to be at least seven or eight metres, simply unbelievably huge, and at least twice as long as our dinghy. We gave it a wide berth, but having survived the shooting era, it was more frightened of us than we were of it – Jacquie excepted. We knew it was the younger crocs

that we had to worry about because they had grown up in an era when man no longer presented a threat. They were absolutely fearless and it was quite common for them to hang around the dinghy when we were fishing or to snap up the filleted carcasses. In Arnhem Land and the Kimberleys, there is no swimming at all because of the crocs. Even walking close to water presents a constant risk. Once I was walking along a beach heading back to the dinghy when a four-metre croc tore across my path, about five metres away. It must have been sunbaking and was heading to the water. Seeing it ploughing through the sand at top speed was frightening.

Still, that's life in the Kimberleys. You never know what you'll find. We paid a visit to an abandoned World War II air force base where we came across some antiquated bulldozers and dusty old trucks, one of which looked as if it might still work. Nick used his penknife to get the truck going, and we hopped in and roared up and down the airstrip as the vehicle belched huge clouds of black smoke. What we didn't know was that the truck belonged to someone. After the film was shown on TV, its owner threatened to sue me, but I think he was less upset than embarrassed at the hard time he got from his mates for letting his truck spew out so much smoke.

On the other side of the peninsula we came across the remnants of a crashed plane, which looked to be from World War II. Seeing the plane in the jungle brought back memories of an earlier trip to the Solomon Islands. We had cruised into Baroke Harbour, scene of a lot of action during the war in the Pacific, and came across a sunken Japanese freighter, its masts still sticking up above the surface. I moored our boat by securing fore and aft lines to the masts and we went ashore to an old gun emplacement. As we were looking around, Trina Fleischmann spotted a Japanese warplane crashed in the jungle. One of the famous Mitsubishi Zeros, it was still in excellent condition. Trina pulled away some branches and climbed onto the wing to look inside. What she saw made her scream: the skeleton of the pilot still strapped in his seat.

Such is my life. You never know what is behind the branches or around the next bend.

My son Dean with two sizeable barramundi he had just speared.

An adventurer's life

I WAS NOT AN ADVENTUROUS CHILD. I wasn't the sort who wandered off or fought against his parents' authority. I was just an ordinary kid who lived a simple, active life at Lennox Head, which sowed the seeds of my love for the outdoors. That love is every bit as strong today as it was the day I first pulled on my homemade mask and discovered a whole new world under the sea.

Looking back on 55 years of diving and 45 years of filmmaking makes me realise just how lucky I was to be born when I was. In my early days of diving, I saw reefs and fish populations that were virgin. I was the first person to see them and they will never be seen that way again. The plethora of fish and underwater life I could access so easily when I was young simply do not exist in such numbers any more. My own sons can never witness the unspoilt territory I was so lucky to see.

At the same time, I was fortunate to live in an era when technology made it possible to dive deeper, explore further and record what I saw on film to be beamed into households around the world.

When I first learned to dive it was simply an experience I enjoyed. I could not imagine that one day I would be able to educate and excite people by sharing my adventures.

There will never be another era like it. The freedom to explore which divers of my time enjoyed so much will never return. In recent years, walls of bureaucratic regulations and restrictions have become the bane of my life. In the early days, I used to think the most difficult part of filmmaking was working with wildlife and capturing special moments on film. Now the hardest part is getting through the red tape to get close to the wildlife in the first place.

Australia has become an over-regulated country. Laws have been put in place to stop bad people, but all too often those with good intentions also suffer. I have lost count of the number of times I have been hindered by the "little kings", the bureaucrats, government officials and over-zealous park rangers, who follow the letter of the law at the expense of common sense.

 *A tiger shark homes in on marlin bait. Photo by Lynn Cropp on board the* Beva.

The butterfly fish, right, is a common beauty encountered in shallow reef waters. Below, my catch of the day, a "red", aka a large-mouth nannygai. or sea perch. They can reach 1m long and weigh up to 14kg.

Of course I believe that conservation and protection of the environment are vital, but to erect too many barriers can be counter-productive. The best tool to encourage conservation is education, not over-regulation. And the best way to educate is to permit access to threatened areas and species for a selection of qualified filmmakers, who can take the message to the world.

For most of my life, it has been my great good fortune to be in that position. I have also enjoyed success and good health. I have been able to live the dream I had as a young man, to follow in the wake of my hero, Hans Hass, pioneer diver and filmmaker.

Just as he inspired me, it is gratifying to know that I have been able to inspire others to follow a similar life. When young people tell me my films encouraged them to become divers or explorers or even just to travel to unusual destinations, I feel proud.

The feeling is the same when my peers honour my work. In 2000, I travelled to the Cayman Islands to be admitted into the International Scuba Divers Hall of Fame.

At the time I was only the 19th inductee, joining people such as Jacques Cousteau, Lloyd Bridges, Ron and Val Taylor and, of course, Hans Hass. Sadly, many of those pioneers are no longer with us, but Lloyd Bridges' daughter was at the ceremony as was the man who nominated me, Cousteau's son Jean-Michel Cousteau.

To be in such lofty company is a great honour and the ultimate accolade for that decision I made all those years ago to walk away from a steady job as a schoolteacher with youthful confidence that my future lay somewhere over the horizon. I know I have made mistakes, particularly in my love life. I have had three wives, Van, Eva and Lynn, who have shared my passion with me. I made eight films with Eva and more than 45 with Lynn, and we all still call each other friends, which means we must have been doing something right. More recently, I have shared my life and adventures with Lynn Roberts and Trina Fleischmann, who have been a great support and good shipmates. I have raised two fine sons and seen things I could never have imagined.

My life has been an adventurous one and I know there are plenty of things still to do and plenty of places still to see. Antarctica has always interested me, but I never found time to get there.

Now I've booked my tickets. My bag is always packed and my camera close by. Old pirates like me never retire. We just keep sailing off over the horizon, to see what we can see.

Glossary

Shark facts

• Over 200 years of Australian records (at the time of writing this book) there have been 192 deaths from shark attacks (Qld 72; NSW 71; SA 21; WA 13; Vic 7; NT 3; Tas 5).

• An average of 1.3 Australians die each year from shark attacks. According to the Australian Shark Attack File, in the past 20 years, deaths have been as follows: SA 11; Qld 7; WA 6; NSW 1; Tas 1; Vic 0; NT 0. Only about one-third of shark attacks are fatal. Twice as many people die from a bee-sting, and many, many more from water-related accidents unconnected to sharks.

• Of more than 450 species worldwide, 166 are found in Australian waters. All sharks are protected, and only a handful are regarded as dangerous to humans.

• Proven man-eaters:
White shark (white pointer) *Carcharodon albimars*
Tiger shark *Galeocerdo cuvieri*
Whaler shark *Galeolamna macrurus*
 (includes the Bull shark).

• Potentially dangerous to humans:
Wobbegong *Orectolobus maculatus*
Hammerhead *Orectolobus* sp.
Blue shark *Prionace glauca*
Mako *Isurus* sp.
Grey nurse shark *Odontaspis arenarius*

WHITE SHARK
Carcharodon albimars
(alias Great White, White Pointer, White Death)

Identified in fatal unprovoked shark attacks on humans in Australia.
The largest and most ferocious species, the white shark can grow to at least 6m in length and weigh 3,000kg. Blue-grey or bronze above and stark white below, its body is torpedo-shaped, with pointed snout, large fins, crescent-shaped tail, black eyes and large serrated teeth.
Found in temperate, coastal waters from southern Queensland to the north-west of Western Australia. Evidence suggests numbers are decreasing.
Adult white sharks eat seals, sea lions, dolphins and dead whales, some also eat fish such as snapper. Known to eat elephant seals, sea otters, turtles and sea birds.

TIGER SHARK
Galeocerdo cuvieri

Identified in fatal unprovoked shark attacks on humans in Australia.
The tiger shark grows to at least 6m, has a blunt head, serrated teeth in a cockscomb formation, and a slender body with vertical bands of darker colouring that can fade with age. Its large size and its habits of scavenging and feeding in shallow waters make it dangerous to humans.
Found in tropical and some subtropical waters from the south-west of Western Australia around the tropical north and east coast as far as central NSW.
The tiger shark can produce as many as 47 pups.
Material found in tiger shark stomachs has included:
• dogs
• sea birds
• half a dolphin
• a handbag containing a watch (still ticking)
• an iron pot

- a ship's chain
- a bulldog (with a rope around its neck)
- a horse

WHALER SHARK
Galeolamna macrurus

Identified in fatal unprovoked shark attacks on humans in Australia.

Whalers are a large group of sharks (never to be confused with whale sharks) found all around Australia; in Queensland there are probably more than 17 species, and they can be difficult to identify. They vary in size from bait-stealers less than a metre long to big 4.3m man-eaters.

Most common of the larger Queensland species implicated in attacks on humans is the Bull Shark. The Bull shark is known to enter freshwater rivers and lake and has been responsible for fatal attacks in the man-made channel system around the Gold Coast in recent years. In colour it is grey above and cream below and can grow to over 3 metres in length.

The bronze whaler (*carcharhinus brachyurus*) favours south Queensland seas. It can grow to 2.7 metres and is bronze and cream in colour.

GREY NURSE SHARK
Odontaspis arenarius

A sluggish species, the Grey Nurse is not usually considered dangerous to people, but divers should never provoke it.

Sometimes said to be named for its ability to corral small fish into a tight school for feeding, it grows up to 3.6m and is usually grey-brown on top and dirty white underneath. Its fang-like teeth are visible even when its mouth is closed.

Found in temperate waters, it has been recorded in all states of Australia except Tasmania. It is the most critically endangered of Australian marine species, and was the first to become protected.

WHALE SHARK
Rhincodon typus

A harmless giant, it is docile, but can be a hazard to small craft. Named for its bulk and its habit of eating plankton, but unrelated to the whale, the whale shark is the largest of all sharks, reaching more than 15m. It's easy to recognise because of its huge size, wide, spade-like head, long ridges from head to tail and domino-like pale spots between. It has more than 250 rows of tiny, sandpaper-like teeth and feeds on the surface on small crustaceans, other plankton and occasionally little fish. Whale sharks constantly emit a faint croaking noise, thought to be a form of sonar. It's usually found in the open ocean waters of Queensland, at 9m-12m depths. It is considered endangered.

TAWNY SHARK
Nebrius ferrugineus
(alias Tawny Nurse shark, Madame X, Rusty shark, Sleepy shark, Spitting shark)

The tawny shark has a broad, flattened head, square snout, tiny eyes and large fins, and is coloured in shades of brown to grey. It can grow to more than 3m, and is found in tropical areas, often inshore or near reefs, in Western Australia, the Northern Territory and Queensland. It is nocturnal and docile, and feeds on octopus, fish and crabs. Credited with a few provoked attacks, during which it is said to bite and hang on.

LEMON SHARK
Negaprion brevirostris

This large reef shark, which is pale yellow to brown on top, and lighter yellow below, can grow up to 3.5m. Usually solitary and found in subtropical waters and around reefs, it feeds on bony fish. Worldwide, it has been involved in several attacks on humans.

Other dangerous creatures

QUEENSLAND GROPER
Epinephelus lanceolatus
(alias Giant Grouper)

Implicated in fatal attacks on humans, the Queensland groper has a large mouth and rounded tail. The young have irregular black and yellow markings, the adults are green-grey to grey-brown with faint mottling and small black spots on fins. The largest fish on coral reefs, this groper can grow to at least 2.7m and more than 400kg. A voracious, fearless feeder, it often lives in submarine caves or the wreckage of sunken ships, so can be vulnerable to spearfishing.
Found from the southern coast of WA, around the tropical north to the southern coast of NSW.

SEA SNAKE
Hydrophis elegans
(alias Elegant Sea Snake)

Not to be confused with reef eels, which can be vicious biters, the sea snake is venomous (10 times more so than a cobra). Not all sea snake bites cause poisoning. Unlike the eels, sea snakes have a flattened, stiff tail like a paddle and a scaly body.
Found in Australian coastal waters and estuaries from tropical WA through Torres Strait right around to Queensland, NSW and central Victoria, one of the commonest varieties is the Elegant sea snake, which grows to more than 2.1m. Left undisturbed, sea snakes are not aggressive.

BRYDE'S WHALE
Balaenoptera edeni
(alias Tropical whale)

Long and more streamlined than other large whales, the Bryde's whale is dark grey with a yellowish-white underside. They weigh from 12,000 to 20,000 kg and their average length is 12m, although they can reach 15.5m. (At birth they weigh up to 1,000 kg and measure about 4m.) Instead of teeth, they have two rows of plates on the top jaw, 300 per side. They live for at least 50 years.
Bryde's whales are non-migratory and found worldwide in temperate and subtropical waters. They have been recorded throughout Australian waters, except the Northern Territory, with concentrations off Queensland and off the west coast. They feed mostly on shoaling fish such as anchovies, and often ruin other predators' tea parties by swimming through and engulfing fish they have herded.
Bryde's whales are protected, and world estimates are 40,000 to 80,000. They are at risk from seismic operations, entanglement in fishing gear, pollution and over-fishing of their food stock. An inquisitive species, they often approach boats, and collisions sometimes result (one with a large vessel is recorded in Tasmanian waters and another off northern NSW).

SALTWATER CROCODILE
Crocodylus porosus
(alias Estuarine crocodile, "Saltie")

The world's largest reptile in terms of bulk, saltwater crocodiles can reach 6-7m and up to 1,000kg. Females are much smaller. They have a large head, heavy jaws and a greatly prized scaly skin, which is dark-coloured with lighter tan and grey areas. They can have up to 68 teeth.
Able to tolerate saltwater, this species is found in brackish water in rivers and coastal areas, but also in freshwater rivers, billabongs and swamps.
There are estimated to be more than 100,000 in northern Australia, but numbers are depleted elsewhere (except in PNG). They produce 40-60 eggs, but it's estimated that fewer than one per cent of hatchlings reach maturity.
The adult eats mudcrabs, turtles, snakes and water birds. Larger models have been known to eat buffalo, domestic animals and wild pigs. They kill or injure a number of humans each year.

FRESHWATER CROCODILE
Crocodylus johnstoni
(alias Johnston's crocodile, "Freshie")

A smaller crocodile, that rarely reaches more than 2.5-3m. It has a narrow, tapered snout with up to 72 sharp teeth, and large scales.
Found in lakes, billabongs and swamps, and in the upper reaches of rivers and creeks in WA, NT and Qld. The population is thought to number more than 50,000.
The "freshie" eats fish, invertebrates and smaller vertebrates. On average, the female lays 13 eggs, but only a third will hatch, and less than one per cent reach maturity.
At risk from habitat destruction and cane toads.

BOX JELLYFISH
Chironex fleckeri
(alias Sea Wasp, "Stinger", Fire Medusa, Indringa)

They are found along the northern coast of Australia from Gladstone in the east to Exmouth in the west. The other large species, *Chiropsalmos*, has been found only in the Cairns area. Stinger season in the top of Australia begins with the wet season about October and lasts until April. Further south the season is usually December until March. Box jellyfish are usually found in shallow waters along beaches.
The largest species of jellyfish, *Chironex fleckeri* is one of the world's most dangerous creatures. It is pale blue and transparent and bell-shaped, weighing up to 6kg and measuring up to 30cm across the bell. Its tentacles at each corner of the "box" can stretch more than two metres and can number 60 in total. Each tentacle contains millions of nematocysts (stinging cells) which discharge venom through the skin on contact, causing excruciating pain, breathing problems, cardiac arrest, lesions, and often death within minutes.
Box jellyfish eat fish and small invertebrates, which they spy with 48 eyes.

IRUKANDJI
Carukia barnesi

A tiny jellyfish barely 2cm across found in northern Australia, especially north Queensland. Found in deeper waters of the Great Barrier Reef, although sometimes swept inshore by currents. Stings have been recorded from Childers to Broome.
Every summer 60 people are hospitalised after being stung by irukandji. Initial pain is moderate, but followed within half an hour by a syndrome of symptoms that include severe back or abdominal pain, nausea and vomiting.

The migrants

CHRISTMAS ISLAND RED CRAB
Gecarcoidea natalis

It's estimated 120 million of these big, bright-red land crabs – the adult shell can measure 116mm across – live on Christmas Island. At the beginning of the wet season (usually October/November), the adults suddenly begin a spectacular synchronised migration from forest to coast, to breed and release eggs into the sea. The males reach the coast first to dig burrows where the mating occurs. The eggs are released as the high tide turns during the last quarter of the moon. Migration can take 18 days, and thousands of crabs are crushed crossing roads. "Crab crossings" are being built under roads that cross main migration paths.

Acknowledgements:
We are grateful for the assistance of:

Taronga Zoo (Shark Attack File)
Website: www.zoo.nsw.gov.au

Australian Museum
Website: www.amonline.net.au/